Orange Sunshine

How I Almost Survived
America's Cultural Revolution

Marc DuQuette

ORANGE SUNSHINE

ISBN: 978-0-9798529-0-9

Dedicated to

Madame Sonia Rosinka

ACKNOWLEDGEMENT

I want to acknowledge my great gratitude to Martha Theus and Kamaal Theus! Martha, for guiding me every step of the way in presenting *Orange Sunshine: How I Almost Survived America's Cultural Revolution* to the world and for the wonderful YouTube interviews we did together. Kamaal, thank you for designing the cover of my book, which exceeded my wildest dreams! You two are awesome!

Marc DuQuette

ORANGE SUNSHINE

HOW I ALMOST SURVIVED AMERICA'S CULTURAL REVOLUTION

MARC DUQUETTE

TABLE OF CONTENTS

ONCE UPON A TIME

Dad was not a religious man. Mom accused him of being an Atheist. She once whispered to me, in a conspiratorial tone-of-voice, that Darwin's *Origin of Species* was his Bible. Naturally, I wanted to be an Atheist and read Charles Darwin. I wanted to be just like my dad. Thus, I was very surprised by what he asked me to do.

I had just gotten home from school, and was in the kitchen looking for a snack. Dad was on his way to work. He paused on his way out the door, and squatted down eye-level to me. He smelled of cigarettes and appeared very somber.

"Son, the little boy who lives in back of us is real sick. His mom accidentally slammed his hand in the car door. The doctors fixed his hand but he hurt it again. He was playing in his yard and got dirt and dog poop under his bandages. The wound got infected, and he's back in the hospital. The doctors don't think he'll live. He's got lockjaw. Would you please pray for him, son? God listens to you".

Dad stood up, grabbed his black metal lunch box, and without another word, went off to his job in the oil fields. I was eight years old and had no idea why my dad thought, "God listens" to me. I didn't know what tetanus was. I visualized a little boy lying in a hospital bed with a huge lock around his jaw. I silently prayed,

"God, if it be your will, please let the little neighbor boy live. Amen." I didn't know the kid. I thought my prayer was very half-assed and insincere.

Several days later, I overheard Mom and another neighbor talking about the little boy. They said he was making a full recovery and would be home soon. Dad never again spoke of his prayer request, so I haven't mentioned it until now.

Chapter 1

MOTORCYCLE DOWN

The pint of tequila I had for lunch was completely metabolized, but the Benzedrine was still pumping through my system. I was feeling very good, as if my soul was too big for my body.

One of my biker friends and I were headed south out of Santa Ana. It was the night before Halloween 1966, and I was on my way home from work.

Skosh was riding his ancient rigid frame Harley chopper, and I was on my modified Norton.

The Norton had started out as a shiny new 750 Scrambler. Now it was a 750 cubic inch Norton engine shoehorned into a super lightweight BSA racing frame. A Norton chopper was a very unique motorcycle, even in Southern California. It was beautiful, clean, and too fast for me!

My long hair and beard were blowing in the wind. I liked the way my Mexican *serape* billowed behind me, like a colorful cape.

Dusk had just turned to night. The cool air felt good on my face. My mind was filled with important thoughts: "Maybe I should stop at the Buccaneer Bar for a pitcher of beer on my way home. I sure do like Skosh's suicide clutch. I wonder if I could convert the

Norton's transmission to something similar…Wow, the car ahead of me doesn't have any taillights." I pulled alongside the driver's side, turned my head for an instant, and yelled, "Hey lady, your taillights are out!" In that moment, the station wagon directly ahead of *her* changed into my lane and stopped abruptly.

I didn't have time to apply the brakes, and plowed into the rear of the station wagon at about forty miles an hour.

My crotch went into and over the motorcycle's gas tank, lacerating both testicles on the chrome ridge of the gas cap. The gas tank was ripped off the frame. Thirty coats of hand-rubbed red lacquer had recently been applied to that tank!

After making a brief pause in the handlebars, I flew headfirst completely over the stopped station wagon.

My forehead and nose slammed into the pavement. I heard a "crunch- splat!" sound explode inside my head. I knew I was in serious trouble.

I instinctively jumped up and rolled off the pavement, onto the shoulder of the road, so I wouldn't be in traffic.

My head and face were numb, but my nuts hurt. Skosh witnessed the crash and ran over to try to keep me from thrashing around. He also moved my wrecked bike off the road. The engine was the only thing that wasn't destroyed.

My custom racing frame was bent like a pretzel. All that chrome plate and hand-rubbed lacquer, gone. The tiny uncomfortable seat, the buddy pad behind it, the sissy bar with the provocative Iron Cross welded onto it, the custom exhaust system that rattled car windows when I blasted down the freeway – all destroyed in an instant!

An ambulance arrived within minutes. I never lost consciousness, but I wanted to.

The Santa Ana police were on the scene to direct traffic and investigate the crash. Cops and paramedics asked me endless dumb questions. "Why is the *man* hassling me? I just want to go to sleep". I learned later they were just trying to keep me awake due to the head injury. They were concerned I would slip into a coma.

I didn't answer their questions, but repeatedly asked them if my nuts were okay! Finally, one of the ambulance guys said, "Yeah, but you're going to require some stitches".

I really wanted to drift off into unconsciousness, but they wouldn't let me, and that made me irritable.

I don't remember much about the ride to the hospital or the check-in procedure, but I was in the operating room over three hours – wide-awake the whole time! When it was all over, they told me I had needed 140 stitches in my head and face, and several more to stitch-up my balls. That part really hurt!

My poor nose was really pulped-out from the impact with the pavement. I'll never forget the crunching sound as they straightened and set my nose.

My life truly did flash before my eyes that night on the operating table. It was similar to the near death experiences people talk about, except no tunnel, no smiling relatives, no white light.

I didn't care for my life review. I saw a twenty-four year old man full of ego and self-interest - a jerk. Specific examples of my jerkness were presented to my consciousness.

I mentally, but tearfully, told God I'd make a real effort to be a better person. No deals, just regret, remorse and a desire to be a better man.

Miraculously, I only needed to spend a few days in the hospital. On Halloween, a few of my biker buddies came to visit me in my hospital room. They joked about my not needing a scary mask. My forehead was covered with stitches and two long rows of stitches bracketed my smashed nose. I had two black eyes, which took months to fade to normal skin color. I looked worse than I felt. We didn't talk about my nuts, but they healed quickly and completely.

My biker buddies brought me a pint of vodka and a baggie of pot. I ate the marijuana and washed it down with the booze while my friends stood around me, blocking the nurses' view.

The day before I was released from the hospital, my eighteen-year-old brother, Lon, came to visit me. He looked very strange. He was giggling and mumbling. Irritated by his lack of somberness for my predicament, I asked him what the fuck was going on. He mumbled, "I took some LSD last night."

I became very interested, having just read about two Harvard psychologists named Leary and Alpert. They had been experimenting with LSD, and enthusiastically promoted it's use.

Lon told me his experience with the drug was very positive and said, "You'll like it, but it's nothing like pot, or alcohol, or whites. It's really different!"

Lon appeared very excited about his experience. I was a little wary, because along with Leary and Alpert's rave reviews of the drug, I'd also heard stories of suicides, kids going blind staring at the sun, and cases of permanent psychosis.

I had also read about people having flashbacks of traumatic experiences from their past while under the influence of LSD. I could imagine experiencing my motorcycle wreck again and again, like a hellish episode of the *Twilight Zone*.

Sometimes, even now, I think I may still be on the operating table, dying. My will to live is so strong that I'm mentally projecting or imagining a post-motorcycle-wreck life. What has seemed to me to be more than forty years may really be taking place in my last few moments of life in a hospital in Santa Ana on Halloween Eve 1966.

Chapter 2

BORN IN A BLACKOUT

I was born July 23, 1942 at three-thirty in the morning, wartime in Long Beach, California. My mom told me I was "three weeks late", and my dad said I looked "all beat up" when I was delivered – two black eyes and lots of bruises. I know I didn't want to be here.

Pearl Harbor had been attacked only six months previously, and Japanese submarines were reported to be off the coast of California. Long Beach was a prime military target. A large naval base and major oil fields were located in Long Beach, and a huge ammunition storage facility was nearby at Seal Beach. Weapons of mass destruction were rumored to be stored there.

Due to wartime conditions, Long Beach was often "blacked-out" at night. I was born in a blackout, which just meant all windows had to be covered with blackout shades and automobile headlights had to be dimmed.

My earliest memories are of being afraid of the Japanese. My dad worked in the oil fields between Seal Beach and Huntington Beach. He was a "driller" and worked long hours and rotating shifts. I was afraid the Japanese would blow up the oil fields at night when my dad was at work.

ORANGE SUNSHINE

We lived in a tiny apartment in the city of Long Beach until I was nearly six years old, and my mom was pregnant with my brother, Lon.

I was the first-born. My mom was neurotic and needy, and my dad was either working (sometimes double-shifts), or trying to sleep. This was not a good thing. As soon as I was able to talk, I was forced into the role of my mom's confidant. I was also the poor soul she took out all her anger and frustration upon. Looking back with today's understanding, I was truly a physically and emotionally abused child – until my brother was born.

Several months before Lon was born, we moved to Lakewood, a brand new working class suburb of Long Beach. Lakewood was a community of low-cost single family homes with real front yards and real backyards!

Cornfields and the old oil fields of Signal Hill separated Lakewood from the city of Long Beach. Nearby, Long Beach Airport and the adjacent Douglas Aircraft manufacturing complex were gearing up for the Korean War.

My mom's physical abuse of me continued in Lakewood until Lon was born, and then it stopped completely. Looking back at my early childhood, I cannot connect a beating to a behavior that would justify such harsh punishment.

Lon was born July 11, 1948 in Long Beach. Mom and Lon had to stay in the hospital about five days after his birth.

Dad was still working lots of overtime and rotating shifts in the oil fields, so a lady was hired to look after me while Dad was at work. I was a few days from my sixth birthday. The main thing I remember about the lady was the lumpy cream of wheat she cooked for me every day. At least Mom made it smooth.

The day Dad brought Mom and Lon home from the hospital, my caregiver held Lon, looked at him deeply, and said in a spooky dramatic voice, "I wonder who he was in his previous life"

Mom freaked out and fired her on the spot. The poor lady did seem like a character from *Rosemary's Baby*.

Chapter 3

LIQUOR STORE WONDERLAND

My parents were close friends to an elderly couple who owned a liquor store in downtown Long Beach. Cora and Clarence lived in an apartment connected to, and at the rear of the liquor store. Their twenty-eight year old son, Arthur, lived in a small trailer parked in the rear of the liquor store/apartment. I was about seven or eight years old at the time.

I was fascinated by Clarence and Arthur, but was somewhat afraid of them, too. The father and son each had several fingers missing. As young as I was, I was smart enough to think (in kids' language),"genetics" or "heredity", maybe? I asked my dad about it. He said, "dynamite", and wouldn't say any more about it. Dad was like that.

Fascinated as I was with Clarence and Arthur and their missing fingers, I was *obsessed* with the liquor store.

Whenever our family visited Cora and Clarence in their apartment, I always took the opportunity to dreamily walk around the interior of the liquor store. I was entranced by the multicolored bottles and the magic elixirs they contained. I tried to memorize the "proof" of the contents of each bottle, not consciously knowing what "proof" meant. I lovingly touched each bottle I could reach. The glass bottles felt cool to the touch, in contrast to the hot, unairconditioned store.

One night, for a reason I can't remember, I had to sleep overnight at Cora and Clarence's liquor store/apartment. They put me up for the night on a little cot in Arthur's trailer.

Arthur got up from his bed about every hour and drank whiskey straight out of the bottle. The smell of alcohol filled the tiny trailer. I could actually *feel* his withdrawal anxiety before he took each drink; then, I could *feel* him relax as the alcohol took effect. I thought to myself, "Arthur must be sick and the whiskey makes him feel better, but it's also the whiskey that makes him sick – fascinating."

Arthur died of alcoholism several months later.

Chapter 4

ARMING MYSELF

I was the man of the house when Dad worked swing and graveyard shifts. Frequently, in the middle of the night, Mom heard noises in the house. She would wake me up and make me search the dark house to make sure there were no intruders. I don't know why she didn't just let me turn on all the lights. I didn't have a flashlight, and was really scared – especially when checking the closets.

Oil workers were tough, wild guys. My dad was the working foreman of a crew of "roughnecks". One time he had to fire one of the guys on his crew, and the man actually came to our house in the middle of the night while Dad was at work. He didn't get into our house, but I heard he came over to terrorize our family. The police watched our home all night. I don't remember how the incident was resolved. I was about eight years old at the time, but I felt responsible for protecting Mom and my two-year-old brother.

Mom and Dad were anti-gun, but through the strength of my eight-year-old will, I convinced them to buy me a B.B. pistol. I was a natural with it -- naturally safe and naturally responsible. With a little practice, I became quite an accurate shot as well. The following year, I bought a Daisy B.B. rifle. At age eleven, I talked my parents into buying me a Mossberg .22 bolt action rifle with a tubular magazine, sling, and telescopic sight. I had seen this rifle advertised and pictured in the Sears or Montgomery Wards catalog, and fantasized about it for months.

I convinced my mom to drive me to the police shooting range, where cops and interested citizens taught me firearms safety, marksmanship, and the care and cleaning of my rifle. I've owned firearms ever since.

Chapter 5

BURNING THE EASTER BUNNY

I got along well with the neighborhood kids my age. We explored the as yet undeveloped areas of Lakewood, and ventured as far as Signal Hill. We played cowboys, cops and robbers, Nazis and Americans – the usual stuff. Cap guns, squirt guns, and relatively safe dart guns were involved. We couldn't find any toy German Lugers, but we had some very cool cap guns.

As Lon and I got a little older, I tried to bring him into the games a bit. By the time he was three and I was nine, we were playing with my cap guns. I let him watch, from a safe distance, as I blew up plastic model cars with firecrackers. We didn't play destructively with my B.B. guns, however. For some reason I was super cautious and responsible with them.

It's hard to believe now, but in the early 1950s, every home in Lakewood had an incinerator in the back yard. Ours was behind the garage.

As far as I know, at that time everyone burned their trash in their own backyards. Smog was really thick in those days. Sometimes I could hardly breathe.

I loved to burn the trash! I remember milk cartons were especially interesting to watch burn. Milk cartons were coated with a waxy substance that bubbled and sizzled as the carton melted and burned.

I also loved to collect and stash money here and there. Lon had a huge stuffed Easter bunny. It was old, beat up, and had a hole in it, into which I stuffed a few dollars and change. Months later, I decided the Easter bunny was dead and must be cremated in the incinerator. Lon didn't care about the old stuffed toy anymore, so he agreed the bunny should burn. With great ceremony and dignity, we carried the Easter bunny to the incinerator and fired it up.

As the bunny began to burn, I remembered there was money in it! With shrieks of imagined terror, we had to rescue the now living but hideously burning bunny from the flames. We pulled it from the fire and turned the garden hose on it.

Miraculously, the bunny and the money were saved. The resurrected Easter bunny was slightly scarred from the experience, but it gave him character. We kept him until Mom finally threw him out.

Chapter 6

HORIZONTAL BARS

My dad was a locally famous athlete when he was a kid growing up in Long Beach in the 1920s. Dad was a track star, gymnast, and high diver. He won medals in these sports in high school. Many of his medals were taken away from him after the school found out he was a member of a professional athletic association. I think he was bitter his whole life about that, as he was never a *paid* professional athlete.

I believe because his athletic career was thwarted, he projected onto me his desire for athletic success. So we tried softball, baseball, and football – unsuccessfully. Dad, with his penetrating Scorpio intuition, was also very likely tuning-in to my alcoholic personality and trying to channel my energies into athletics.

When I was about ten years old, Dad came home from his job in the oil fields, probably drunk. He dug postholes, poured concrete, and installed Olympic class horizontal bars in the backyard. When the concrete was set, he proceeded to give me a demonstration of how to use the bars, gracefully swinging from bar to bar, finishing the exercise with a back flip that was so high and tight, he could have probably done a double flip. He was truly a humble man, so he only did a single flip. I was supposed to grasp it all from observing this demonstration. He never got on the bars again. As time passed, it became obvious the neighborhood kids played on my bars more than I did. I preferred to read sea stories and science fiction, shoot my B.B. gun at toy soldiers, and set model cars on fire or blow them up in the backyard. I made hideous noises as the imaginary villains in the cars burned up!

I did play on the bars, but not enough to satisfy my dad. One day he came home from work really drunk and ripped the bars out of the ground with pick ax and shovel. I cried and pleaded with him not to do it. I promised I would use the bars more often. He didn't pay any attention to my pleas, and I'll never forget the feelings of shame and worthlessness I felt for disappointing my father. I also got in touch right then with some really cold and powerful anger toward him for making me feel such shame.

Chapter 7

JUNIOR HIGH IN LAKEWOOD

I started junior high school in Lakewood when I was twelve years old. Gangs and drugs were not unheard of in 1954 Los Angeles County. Kids talked about the "pachucos". We thought of the pachucos as a huge, loosely knit gang that permeated every *barrio* and Mexican-American neighborhood in the Southwest.

The identifying mark of the pachuco was a small tattoo of a cross, with three rays extending from the top of the cross. The tattoo was located on the hand, between the thumb and forefinger.

Our junior high had over fifteen hundred students. We had a few real pachucos, a number of pachuco wannabees, who drew the tattoo on their hands with ink pens, and some girlfriends of pachucos. Those girls fascinated me. They seemed so mature and sensual.

The pachucos were associated in my mind with the legendary zootsuiters of the World War Two era. I was too young to remember the original zootsuiters, but my dad talked about them – how cool they looked.

Local youth gangs usually confined their little wars to fighting rival gangs. Civilians rarely got caught in the crossfire. "Rumbles" were usually about neighborhood territory. Drug turf wasn't the motivating factor in those days.

Pachucos were rumored to use marijuana, but we rarely heard of heroin or cocaine. Those drugs were associated with jazz musicians and singers such as Bird Parker and Billy Holliday.

Gang members usually fought with fists, knives and chains. A few gangsters carried zip guns that were made in shop class. A zip gun was a very primitive single-shot .22 pistol. They rarely functioned, but looked very intimidating to a kid

One of the most impressive moments in my junior high experience was seeing a real pachuco swaggering down the hall, probably on his way to meet his girlfriend. He was covered with tattoos and had a big moustache. I could see the crude wooden butt of a zip gun tucked into his waistband. This was junior high school in 1955!

The "grown-up" pachucos picked up their junior high girlfriends every day after school. They had the coolest cars! There was an informal hot rod and custom car show every afternoon in front of the school. In my junior high opinion, the classic high-end pachuco car was a chopped 1950 Mercury two-door, completely de-chromed, lowered to the ground all the way around, and painted hot rod black primer.

I was what would later be called a "nerd". I wore glasses since the age of nine, had braces, got good grades, and was terrible at sports. I loved to swim in the ocean at Huntington Beach, and shoot baskets at home in my driveway, but nobody wanted me on their basketball team. I was lazy and uncoordinated. I *was* in the Science Club, and hung around with nerdy kids like myself. We had fun trying to mix chemicals that would explode.

To gain wider social acceptance in junior high school, I had to learn the method of giving the finger "Lakewood style". If one couldn't correctly flip someone off, one was in trouble in Lakewood.

The palm of the right hand faces yourself. All fingers are together, extending straight up into the air. The middle finger remains straight up – no bending of middle finger, whatsoever! The fingers on either side of the middle finger must slide and curl along the middle finger until they are tightly closed. Caution: The two sliding and curling fingers must slide and curl simultaneously.

I practiced for hours to master this technique – keeping my hand hidden under my desk, and using a pencil for support at first.

I can still do it!

By the time I entered the eighth grade I was very comfortable in junior high. I could give the finger correctly. Class work was easy for me. I got along well with the pachuco wannabees. The real pachucos were way out of my class!

During the previous summer vacation, between the seventh grade and the eighth grade, another nerdy kid and I built a scale model replica of the interior of King Tut's tomb. We constructed it out of balsa wood and planned to enter it in the Long Beach Hobby Show. We didn't finish it in time. We got hung up reading the *Egyptian Book of the Dead*, although I didn't understand any of it.

One afternoon, in the second week of the eighth grade, I came home from school to find my favorite teacher and my parents sitting in the living room What kind of trouble was I in? I couldn't recall anything I'd done to cause the teacher to pay a special visit to my parents.

The teacher told me I was going to be placed in a special class for kids who were doing well in their regular classes. He said he came by the house to warn my folks I wouldn't like the new class at first, and would try to make them return me to my old classes. The teacher told us my new class would be more work, but assured my parents I'd adjust.

The teacher was right on all counts. I felt the kids in the new class were much smarter than me. I secretly thought of them as "globeheads".

One boy knew the name of every river in the world; another could do math in his head; several kids were bi-lingual, and one girl could quote classic literature. I could barely keep up with the class work, but I felt affection for the globeheads. We were all such misfits.

My former teacher's prediction came true. I adjusted to the more difficult class, and felt happy in school again. Then, the bottom dropped out.

Our family moved to Nebraska two months prior to me finishing the eighth grade. I had to complete the last semester in Nebraska, and begin high school as a freshman in the ninth grade there.

Chapter 8

MY NEBRASKA CARS

During the winter of 1955-1956, our family moved from Los Angeles County to Columbus, Nebraska.

Before we left California, I had become a big fan of black music, hot rods, and custom cars. There was no black music in 1955 Columbus, Nebraska. The only music on the local radio stations was polka, country, and popular music by Frank Sinatra and Perry Como. Cars were another story. Nebraska kids loved cars.

Two distinct styles of custom cars were popular in Columbus. "East coast" style cars were lowered in the rear. They had fender skirts covering the rear wheels. Some East Coast types had extra radio antennas and mud flaps.

I liked the "west coast" style, of course. West coast cars were either lowered all around, or "dagoed" (like, "San Diego") with the front end lowered and the rear end jacked up. West coast cars were sometimes de-chromed, chopped, channeled, and had high performance engines.

I turned fourteen in July 1956, and immediately went to work for Safeway Stores as a box boy. I worked after school and every Saturday. I lied about my age and told the manager I was sixteen. Soon, I was able to purchase a 1932 Ford five-window coupe that was just beginning to rust away in an old farmer's yard. I spent an entire year completely disassembling the car, with the goal of building a chopped and channeled deuce coupe – a street rod. By the time I was fifteen and a half, I'd burned-out on the deuce and sold it to a real hot-rodder. Now I had my learner's permit and immediately needed a vehicle I could actually drive.

I bought a 1946 Ford coupe from an older kid I worked with at Safeway. He was going back east to college and sold it to me at a bargain price. The forty-six coupe was a very cool car. It had the original flat-head V8 engine with the addition of dual pipes and headers. It really sounded sweet! The car also had a 1939 Ford floor shift transmission, which I really liked. After my sixteenth birthday and the acquisition of my driver's license, I de-chromed the body, filled in all the holes with fiberglass, and painted it hot-rod black primer. I also lowered the front-end four inches, and installed a dual carb manifold with two Stromberg "97" carburetors. This modification increased the horsepower and made me a full-fledged hot-rodder.

I drove that little coupe until I graduated from high school and left for the Army. When I returned to Columbus from the active duty part of my training, I sold the 1946 Ford, and purchased a 1939 Ford coupe. The thirty-nine was previously owned by another hot-rodder. It was powered by a souped-up 1948 Mercury flat-head engine.

The Merc really didn't have the power I wanted, so I pulled that engine and jammed a 324 cubic-inch Oldsmobile engine in its place. The engine conversion was a lot of work, and I didn't have the knowledge, skill, or tools to do it all myself. I hired professionals to do the welding and wiring and the heavy work.

I performed a few modifications on the Olds engine and, when finished, I had the fastest car I had driven, up to that point.

There was one major problem with the 1939 Ford/Olds engine combination. I couldn't run a fan! The engine was so large the fan bumped against the radiator. I couldn't move the radiator forward or the hood wouldn't close. I wanted the hood to close so the engine would be concealed.

My car was a "sleeper". In the late 1950s and early 1960s, many people in Nebraska drove twenty-year-old cars. A stock 1939 Ford coupe was not a rare sight. On the outside, my car looked completely stock and kind of beat-up. The wheels and tires looked stock except for the larger tires in the rear, which gave the car better traction. The trunk lid was wired shut and the rear window was cracked. The custom racing exhaust system was concealed. By simply removing four bolts, I could go from a street legal muffler system to a straight pipe competition exhaust.

I had to drive at least thirty to forty miles an hour to keep the engine from overheating, because of the no fan situation. Most of my driving, therefore, was on the open highways of the great flat state of Nebraska.

I lived to race against guys in brand new cars when they would arrogantly attempt to pass me. I only messed with people who were looking to show off. It was fun to observe the surprise on their faces as would blast past them, rattling and shaking, at speeds exceeding one hundred twenty miles an hour. What a death trap that car was! The only safety equipment I had was a seat belt, which wasn't required, but made me feel better.

I finally sold the thirty-nine and bought a 1959 Triumph TR-3 Roadster. The Triumph was a wonderful car. Not too fast, but I couldn't roll it no matter how hard I tried.

In 1964, I sold the Triumph to get enough money to move back to California. I hadn't seen the Pacific Ocean for eight years, although I dreamed about it every night.

Chapter 9

NEBRASKA BARS AND THE TURKEY FRY

I reached the legal drinking age in Nebraska in July 1963, but had been a regular customer in several bars in town since the age of nineteen. I think the Army had given me enough confidence to walk into a bar and *expect* to be served.

Columbus, Nebraska had a population of about fifteen thousand people, and well over thirty bars or restaurants with liquor licenses. My birthday goal was to drink a twelve ounce bottle of "high point" Schlitz beer in each of these establishments.

I started at eight in the morning, in a little Polish bar near the railroad tracks, and consumed my twenty-fourth and twenty-fifth bottle of Schlitz on the street in front of a Czech-German bar eighteen hours later. My designated driver was my best friend from high school, Dave K. I fell short of my goal by at least five bars, but I certainly did get a chance to hear lots of polka music in Polish, Czech, and German!

My favorite bar in Columbus was Eddie's Bar and Grill, located down by the railroad tracks. Eddie's opened at six in the morning, so I often stopped in for breakfast before work – ham, eggs, and a couple of frosty twenty-ounce schooners of tap beer.

Real winos came into Eddie's at six. One morning, as I was enjoying my breakfast, a wino entered the bar and sat at the barstool next to me. The bartender and the wino did not exchange a word of greeting. The bartender pulled a bottle of muscatel fortified wine off the shelf and filled the wino's glass completely to the brim. I watched this scene very carefully, because the wino's hands were shaking violently and the bartender was grinning fiendishly. The wino clutched the glass with both hands, shaking so badly he spilled half the muscatel on the way to his lips. The bartender (who always called me "sport") looked at me, winked and proclaimed loudly, "a little muskie never hurt nobody!"

Every Tuesday night, the Palm Gardens Bar, down by the railroad tracks, had a "turkey fry". I attended several times, but always felt ill the next day. Turkey "fries" were deep-fried turkey nuts, sliced thin and served with garlic bread.

"*Ja*, you come to turkey fry tonight, Marc?" I had to get pretty drunk to eat turkey nuts!

I moved back home to California in early 1964, and none of my new drinking buddies had ever heard of a turkey fry. They thought I was kidding them. One guy even called a turkey ranch and asked if turkeys really had nuts. The man at the turkey ranch replied, "They do, but we don't save 'em out here".

The bar with the toughest reputation in Columbus was the Pawnee Bar, *across* the railroad tracks, on the south side of town. The day JFK was assassinated, I went to the Pawnee to medicate my confused feelings. A man walked into the crowded bar that night and yelled, "Kennedy got what he deserved!" I left immediately, before the police and ambulance arrived. I didn't especially care for the whole Kennedy Camelot illusion, but what a crazy thing to say! I couldn't believe my ears. Someone told me later, the patrons at the Pawnee threw the man through the plate glass window.

Chapter 10

MASON

My dad was a Thirty-Second Degree Scottish Rite Freemason. As a child, I was fascinated by his Masonic ring. Every time I asked him to explain what the symbols meant, or tell me a little about the Masons, he'd just say, "It's a good organization, son". I could never get anymore information out of him regarding the Masons.

A few days after my twenty-first birthday , I applied for membership in our local Masonic Lodge (Lebanon Lodge #323) in Columbus, Nebraska. My lodge brothers told me I was the youngest man ever to be initiated into that particular lodge. The next youngest guy was in his thirties. I went through the three degrees of the Blue Lodge, and was "raised to the Sublime Degree of Master Mason". The complicated rituals seemed very familiar to me. I could almost remember similar rituals from some distant past. On one occasion I gave Third Degree answers to Second Degree questions during the Fellowcraft Degree ritual. The Master of the Lodge became upset and asked, "Who has been coaching this man on the Third Degree?" I replied I hadn't talked to anyone. The answers just seemed to be appropriate to the questions.

My participation in Freemasonry decreased proportionally to the increase in my consumption of beverage alcohol. Within a year, my shame was so great, I couldn't look my Masonic brothers in the eye. I faded away from the lodge, and eventually stopped paying my dues. Local saloons became my lodge, and my drinking buddies replaced my more wholesome lodge brothers.

Chapter 11

THE BUCCANEER BAR

I moved from Columbus, Nebraska to Costa Mesa, California in April 1964, and quickly found work at a large aerospace factory in Santa Ana. I was hired on as a machinist trainee, de-burring machine parts.

Soon after moving to Costa Mesa, I discovered my home bar. The Buccaneer Bar became my social headquarters immediately! This relationship lasted almost ten years. The "Buc" was owned and operated by a very special old guy about my dad's age. Jack was from the Deep South, and was a member of the John Birch Society. His wife, Nadine, was a fine Christian lady who rarely visited the bar. She seemed to embody the higher qualities of her faith. She was strong, kind, and non-judgmental.

Every day after work, I stopped in at the Buccaneer for a pitcher or two. Friday and Saturday nights, I'd hang out until closing time, and take a six pack to go.

A group of us called ourselves "The Buckaroos". We became a very tight circle of drinking buddies. We all smoked pot and hash, and a few of us also popped uppers, which were called "bennies" in those days. We had a very live-and-let-live attitude.

The hardcore buckaroos were: Jack, Charley D, Jon, Dave, Joe, Kenny, Jerry, Wayne, Lon, and myself.

Charley D was Jack's son. He was about my age and had a degree in anthropology. He sang and played guitar with my brother, Lon, in local bars and clubs. They recorded an album together in the late sixties or early seventies.

Jon was a former firefighter and air traffic controller. He periodically battled with the FAA in an attempt to get re-hired as an air traffic controller. John did a little prospecting and was comfortable around dynamite. He usually had a .38 snub nose or a .45 auto within reach.

Dave was a usually good-natured ex-marine and Vietnam vet. He had black belts in everything and was very scary when he wasn't smiling!

"Hawaiian Joe" was one-half Native American and one-half Anglo. Joe also had served in Vietnam . Joe was ex-Army. He had seen and photographed Buddhist monks setting themselves on fire. I think he had witnessed some other disturbing things as well. One night someone torched the little trailer he lived in. Joe implied the *man* had traced him to Costa Mesa and was warning him to keep his mouth shut about the war.

"Mexican Kenny rode the coolest-looking chopper in Costa Mesa. He was a very funny, very intelligent guy. Everyone loved Kenny, although he did get into some trouble related to his association with the world's most infamous motorcycle club. The *man* sent Kenny away for a few years, but he came back refreshed and re-charged.

Jerry was a truck driver, and was my best drinking buddy. Jerry was always up for anything, and had a perpetually cheerful attitude. We called him "One Punch Jerry" because of his tendency to blindside his opponents with one punch. Barroom fights were rare at the Buccaneer. We Buckaroos considered ourselves philosophers, tortured souls, and unemployed soldiers of fortune – not barroom brawlers.

Now and then, Jon and Jerry would get drunk and fight each other. This action took place in the Buccaneer parking lot, and usually ended in a draw. Once, Dave broke Jerry's ribs, but I forget why.

Wayne was a Canadian, with a long red beard. He looked like the big archetypal Scotsman. Wayne was an electrician by trade, but had a very wide range of knowledge on just about any subject.

My brother, Lon and I were also considered full-fledged Buckaroos.

"CIA Jeff" wasn't a real Buckaroo. He hung around the bar and liked to talk to us. He was especially interested in our thoughts about the war. He seemed a little too interested. He was very friendly, always wore Hawaiian shirts, never seemed to have a job, and handled himself well physically. That's why we called him, "CIA Jeff"! He abruptly stopped coming in and no one ever saw him again. We figured we weren't interesting enough.

I drank at the Buccaneer every day, and shared my pot and bennies whenever I was "holding".

My early years at the Buccaneer were my biker years. When I first appeared at the "Buc" in 1964, I was riding a Honda 305 Super Hawk. I quickly sold it and purchased a new 750 Norton, which I later customized into a very unique chopper.

I was a big fan of traditional blues, and went to Los Angeles whenever any of my favorite artists were in town. I was obsessed with the blues. As a kid in Nebraska in the mid-fifties, I would lie awake at night and listen to late night blues and gospel stations originating in the Deep South. Lightning Hopkins, Howlin" Wolf, Bobby Bland, Clifton Chenier, Albert King and John Lee Hooker were my heroes. I listened to Sunday night gospel programs, featuring the Reverend C. L. Franklin and his daughter, Little Sister Aretha Franklin, who was my age.

Jack resisted my pressure to put some blues on the jukebox – at least some B.B. King or Muddy Waters – but he refused.

The regular customers at the Buccaneer were polarized when it came to drugs other than alcohol. Most of the customers didn't approve of drugs. We didn't want any trouble with Jack, or with the Costa Mesa Police Department, so we developed a very silly and transparent code.

Jack had an old pickup truck permanently parked in the lot behind the bar. Whenever we wanted to let the other Buckaroos know we were going outside to smoke some pot or hash, we announced we were going out back to "look at the pickup". We pretended we were thinking about buying it! Of course, everyone knew what we were doing and it became a joke.

This *was* the mid-sixties, and people were doing hard time for possession of even a joint of marijuana. So it was a joke, but it wasn't a joke.

When the Buckaroos started doing LSD in 1966, we called it, "looking at the Big Pickup".

"Wow, you look like you've been looking at the Big Pickup."

Jack sold the Buccaneer in the early seventies. The new owner named it the Country Boy Bar. We were not going to call ourselves the "Country Boys". Some of us drifted down the street and started hanging out at Dick's Horseshoe Saloon. Dick's was a great place! It opened at six every morning, and had a full liquor license.

Dick's Horseshoe was very hardcore. Real criminals frequented the place. The drinks were cheap and strong. If a customer ever got "eighty-six'd" from Dick's, that customer was banned for life. I never saw an exception to that rule. Dick's Horseshoe Saloon became my new home bar, but it never had that cozy, safe feeling of the old Buccaneer.

Chapter 12

GETTING SINCERE AT THE BUCCANEER

A next-door neighbor in my apartment complex turned me on to marijuana in 1964. He was an African-American musician and folk singer. He explained that music sounded better on pot. I was twenty-two years old and had never smoked a cigarette in my life – not even in the Army, where smoking was encouraged. I didn't hesitate, however, when that first joint was offered to me. I just asked, "How do I do this without wasting any?"

A co-worker in the machine shop introduced me to the drug, Benzedrine (amphetamine sulfate) a few months later. Now, my drugs of choice were Benzedrine, marijuana, and alcohol.

Benzedrine was a very powerful, addictive stimulant. I was told, "Long-haul truck drivers use 'em all the time!" Benzedrine tablets, or "bennies", as they were affectionately known, were larger than aspirin tablets, and had crosses on them so they could easily be broken in half, or even in fourths.

Bennies were also called "whites", "white crosses", "uppers", or "*blanquitos*".

Benzedrine really enhanced my drinking. I had a very high tolerance for alcohol, and could consume a large quantity over a long period of time. When I was drunk and wired, I felt I could do anything, knew everything, and really needed to tell everybody everything in a very sincere way.

My source for Benzedrine eventually got fired from the machine shop. I decided to buy them from his source, a drug dealer located just outside the men's room of a bar in Tijuana, B.C., Mexico.

Every few months, I'd make the two and a half hour drive south to Tijuana and score enough for my own personal use, plus a few extra to give to my drinking buddies when they weren't holding up their end of the conversation. I would always try to arrive in Tijuana early in the morning. The streets and bars were as fresh and clean as they would be all day. The strong smell of lysol-soaked mops very nearly covered up the more lusty odors seductively wafting out of the bars.

My little day trips to Tijuana were usually fun adventures. Not many men had long hair and full beards in those pre-hippie days. My dealer always greeted me with, "Hey, Castro! How many you want?" We'd laugh, have a beer, and I would buy my Benzedrine. The bennies were packaged ten tablets to a roll. Each roll was wrapped in aluminum foil. Twenty rolls were packed into Parliament cigarette hard-packs.

In late 1965, I had a scary experience in Tijuana. Several friends from Nebraska were in Costa Mesa visiting me for a few days, taking in the usual tourist attractions. They wanted me to take them to Disneyland and Knott's Berry Farm. I wanted to take them to the Buccaneer and Dick's Horseshoe. They went to Disneyland and met me later at the Buccaneer. After a few pitchers, I suggested we go to Tijuana. "That's a tourist attraction, too!" I pleaded.

I was already secretly wired on bennies that night. My Nebraska friends had no experience with mind/mood affecting drugs other than alcohol. They agreed Tijuana would be fun.

We arrived across the border about ten at night, and hit the bars. The whole time I was thinking this would be a good opportunity to purchase some more bennies. My normal routine was to go to Tijuana in the daytime. I always met the same dealer at the same bar. Now, it was late at night, and we were in unfamiliar bars.

My Nebraska friends started whining about being "tired" around one in the morning. We were all drunk, so I told them about the benefits of Benzedrine. "Hell, all the truck drivers take 'em!" I promised them I could go out on the street and be back in one-half hour with something that would take the tiredness away. They didn't want me to go but I insisted, and left them in the bar to wait for me.

The street was crowded with drunks, pimps, hookers and hustlers of all kinds. I approached a guy I mistook for a cab driver. He was leaning against his car.

"What are you looking for? he asked.

"Blanquitos", I replied.

"How many you want?" he asked

"Dos ciento", I replied.

He flashed some kind of badge, handcuffed me with my hands in front of me, and shoved me into the front passenger seat of his car. He mumbled something about taking me to jail, and started driving. I can't remember what I said, but my limited Spanish expanded into fluency! We seemed to be driving aimlessly, so my alcohol-soaked brain finally figured he just wanted money. I adjusted my body so my wallet pocket became accessible. He stopped the car, reached over and removed my wallet. The "policeman" took all the cash and put the wallet back into my pocket.

"Where you want to go?" he asked.

"Chicago Club", I replied in a shrill voice.

We pulled up in front of the bar, and he removed the handcuffs.

"Blanquitos?" he asked, and pulled a hand full of *rolls* of bennies from his shirt pocket. He was serious. I couldn't believe it! I jumped out of the car and ran into the bar, cold sober and ready to go home.

My Nebraska friends were mad at me for leaving them alone at the bar, and they didn't believe what happened to me. I never returned to Tijuana to buy bennies – ever again.

By divine coincidence, the same musician friend who turned me on to marijuana, introduced me to Benzedrine's more evolved brother, Dexedrine (dextroamphetamine sulfate). He knew a doctor in Colton, California who prescribed it liberally. I loved Dexedrine! It had the same effect as Benzedrine, but didn't make me as jittery.

A few years later, I discovered a doctor in Hollywood who actually provided low cost, high quality uppers from his office. No pharmacy necessary. Every few weeks, I'd drive up to L.A., receive an injection of vitamin B-12, and a "six weeks" supply of uppers.

My typical trip to Hollywood would start from Santa Ana, after my day shift in the machine shop. The doctor's office was near Sunset and LaBrea. I had to sign in, have my weight and blood pressure taken, pay the anorexic receptionist/cashier, and receive my B-12 shot. My uppers were given to me in sealed little white envelopes. Immediately, I'd rip open one envelope, gulp down four or five tablets, and bounce into the cocktail lounge downstairs. After a few too-expensive-for-me drinks, I would hold forth on politics, spirituality, and other "heavy" topics, then leave when I could sense people were becoming irritated with me. Hollywood is about one hour from Costa Mesa, so by the time I walked into the Buccaneer, I was really wired and in need of someone to talk to.

Hawaiian Joe, one of my favorite drinking buddies, also enjoyed the occasional upper with his pitcher of beer. If Joe was in the "Buc" when I returned from Hollywood, we really had fun. I'd pass him a handful of uppers under the bar, and within a half-hour we were telling each other what a great friend the other was. I liked to say, as fast as I could: "YaknowJoeIfeelsogoddamngoodIdontcareifIliveordie!" We called this particular state of consciousness, "getting sincere". In fact, that became our code phrase for getting wired on any upper drug.

"Hey, Joe, wanna get sincere?"

Chapter 13

SNEAKY PETE'S

Shortly after returning to my native California in 1964, and discovering the Buccaneer Bar, I also found Sneaky Pete's in Santa Ana.

My first job in southern California was at Borg-Warner Controls in Santa Ana. I was hired for the most entry-level position in the machine shop, the burr bench. My job was to file and grind the burrs off machined metal parts. The hierarchy of job ratings from bottom to top in the shop was: burr bench, to drill press operator, to milling machine and lathe operator, to "B" Machinist, to "A" Machinist, to Toolmaker. There were no computer-operated machines at that place and time.

De-burring machine parts was hot, dirty work. At the end of an eight to ten hour day shift, a hard-working young man such as myself needed a few cold ones, and perhaps a little excitement.

The Buccaneer Bar in Costa Mesa was only about eight miles from my job in Santa Ana, but I needed a Santa Ana bar, too. I asked my leadman where the "baddest bar in Santa Ana" was located. He did not hesitate a second. "Sneaky Pete's on First and Raitt. You don't want to go there; it's a colored joint and they don't allow white people".

41

I was perched on a barstool in Sneaky Pete's that evening. I connected immediately! The jukebox was full of blues and cool jazz, and the people were very friendly to me.

I was a regular at Sneaky Pete's from 1964 through 1966. I went to the Buccaneer every day, and Sneaky Pete's one or two nights a week.

My behavior at Sneaky Pete's was always respectful, whether I was drunk or less drunk. Most of the other customers were kind to me. We discussed blues, jazz and politics. The name, Patrice Lumumba, came up frequently. I knew enough about the slain African leader to respond appropriately to the various conspiracy theories floating around Sneaky Pete's. "Yeah, I'll bet the *man* had him off'd".

In fact, when I was in the Army in 1960, it was rumored we were going to be sent to the Congo to help the Belgians stop liberation movements in the region.

Every now and then, someone resented my whiteness and would try to start some shit.

"Who's the chuck dude?" someone would ask, referring to me. I thought, "What does that mean? 'Chuck' must be short for 'Charles'. No, "Charlie! "chuck dude" means 'Mister Charlie"!

By the end of that thought process, someone else would diffuse the situation by, "He's cool. He's a gray dude". I took that as a compliment, because the hostility would cease.

On weekends, Sneaky Pete's had live music. I started buying and smoking weed with the musicians, some of whom were also hooked on heroin. I never had the desire to use heroin, but I would ingest tablets or capsules containing opium-based drugs. Any pain medication would do nicely, thank you.

None of my white biker brothers from Costa Mesa wanted to go to Sneaky Pete's with me. They didn't understand why I went there so often. It didn't cross my mind they might be racists. Some of the guys I rode with were in their thirties, and had really been around. A few of them had served time in prison, and had big swastikas tattooed on their arms. I thought the swastikas were just for shock effect. Over time, I realized these guys were serious racists.

One night I was drinking with one of my more moderate biker friends at the Buccaneer. He was crying in his beer that there was no marijuana available in Costa Mesa at the moment. He wanted to get high.

I immediately perked up. "C'mon, let's hop on our scooters and ride over to Sneaky Pete's!"

"Awww, I dunno…"

"It'll be fun. I can score weed for fifty cents a joint. We'll be back at the Buc in an hour!" I was lying about the "in an hour" part.

We jumped on our choppers and roared off into the night. Less than thirty minutes later, we pulled up in front of Sneaky Pete's.

We parked our motorcycles on the sidewalk, near the front door of the bar. The place was full. There was a live band that night, and we got almost as much attention as the band – not all of it positive.

We found a table and ordered some drinks. I excused myself to mix with the crowd until I found my dealer. I was in some favor there because I also used Benzedrine tablets and spread a few around Sneaky Pete's from time to time, as love offerings. I could drink all day and all night on those bennies!

I scored twenty pre-rolled joints from my dealer and returned to our table. My long-haired, bearded, hard-core biker buddy certainly did look extra white sitting there all alone.

"Let's get outta here", he growled.

I shoved the dope deep into the pocket of my Mexican serape, shook hands with a few of my Sneaky Pete's friends, and we blasted out of Santa Ana.

Southbound on Harbor Boulevard, between Santa Ana and Costa Mesa, my outlaw buddy's "peanut tank" ran out of gas. It was now after two in the morning, and we were about a mile from the nearest gas station.

I had an idea. We would position our bodies on our motorcycles so I could extend one leg behind my rear wheel. My buddy could grab hold of my boot. Of course, I couldn't use the rear brake, and I would stay in first gear, but I should be able to tow him into Costa Mesa. With a little effort, we made it work!

In those days, there wasn't much but agricultural land between Santa Ana and Costa Mesa – except for the State Hospital.

As we passed the fenced-in hospital grounds, we saw a police car approaching from a distance. He was coming up on us from behind. We had about ten seconds before he would be upon us.

We stopped our bikes and dismounted. I tried to appear casual as I jammed twenty rolled joints, held together with a rubber band, into my mouth. They all fit, but there wasn't enough room in there to chew and swallow. I gagged them into my hand and pitched them over the fence onto the State Hospital grounds.

The cop either didn't see me do it, or he didn't want the hassle of an investigation on the State Hospital property. He was livid, though!

"What in the hell are you guys trying to do?"

We tried to explain the running out of gas and ingenious towing idea, but the officer was not impressed. He told us we should go to jail, and we would go to jail if we didn't walk our motorcycles into Costa Mesa and park them at the Shell station. Cops were more forgiving about drunk driving in those days.

We expressed our gratitude in the over-the-top, obnoxious, ass-kissing way drunks do when they're not being belligerent or defiantly arrogant.

Several nights later, my biker friend came into the Buccaneer and reported he had climbed the fence at the State Hospital and tried to find the dope. No luck. It made me nauseous to think about it.

Chapter 14

FIRST ACID

Between Thanksgiving and Christmas, 1966, I was home, recuperating from my big pre-Halloween motorcycle crash. I was feeling very disconnected from life.

A small glass jar, containing a capsule of LSD was in my refrigerator. I had been slowly working up the courage to take it.

The day I was scheduled to go back to work, I felt depressed and hopeless. Halfway to the factory, I remembered the capsule in the little glass jar. I made a U-turn, and pointed the nose of my Chevy Malibu home, thinking, "I'm going to take that acid now. I really don't care if I die or go insane. Anything's better than this!"

Returning to my apartment in Costa Mesa, I opened the fridge, grabbed the capsule out of the little glass jar, and swallowed it before I could think about it too much.

I called Lon and told him what I'd done. He said, "Great! I'll be right over". Up to that point I hadn't felt any effects from this "so-called LSD". When Lon arrived minutes later, I was irritated and disappointed.

Lon bounced in cheerfully and suggested I stretch out on the couch. He bustled around the room, adjusted the lights, closed the drapes, and selected a stack of L.P.s. He put the records on the stereo, turned it on, and adjusted the sound. He found a comfortable out-of-the-way chair for himself, and sat quietly reading a book. He had positioned himself so he wasn't looking directly at me.

An album of Bach harpsichord music was playing, as I noticed the light and shadow in the room began to change. The music and the shifting light seemed to be synchronizing.

I started to feel restless. Energy seemed to be moving up my spine. There was a metallic taste in my mouth. I was becoming "experienced". Soon, the walls were breathing; the folds in the drapes became organ pipes filled with maroon-colored fluid. The white cottage cheese ceiling arranged itself into red and green geometrical patterns.

The Bach album changed into the Joan Baez *Noel* album. I was pretty stoned at this point, but remember grasping some realizations before I slipped into the "peak" of the experience, where the conscious mind is incapable of thinking in words.

I "saw" that nothing material is really solid. Matter is energy vibrating at a slower rate. Also, just as many animals can see and hear things we can't, when we are in an altered state of consciousness, we can perceive things we normally aren't aware of.

Everyone knows these things now, but they were deep realizations for a self-centered alcoholic biker to be having in Costa Mesa, California in 1966!

When I re-entered a close imitation of my normal state of consciousness, I thanked Lon profusely, and decided I must do this again very soon.

But first, I had to decide if I needed to cry, giggle, or take a piss.

Chapter 15

BECOMING VEGETARIAN

A few weeks after my introduction to LSD, I attended a "love-in" held in a park in the San Fernando Valley.

I still had the biker mentality and affect, but I was becoming very curious about the hippie movement. It was late 1966, and there weren't many hippies in Orange County, so I began to hang out in Los Angeles on weekends.

I wandered around the park, staring at the hippies in their colorful outfits. Beads, bells, fringy leather shit, flowers in their hair – Really! I wasn't too out of place with my long hair and full beard, but the knife on my belt looked a little harsh.

A hippie girl, wearing a long tie-dyed dress handed me a pamphlet on vegetarianism. I glanced down at it and snapped at her, "Doesn't a carrot *scream* when you pull it out of the ground?" I had recently watched a scientific study on television, which seemed to prove plants could sense pain, danger and fear, as well as love and nurturing. I felt so smug, smarting-off to this gentle young woman. She just smiled in my direction and floated away.

The next weekend, my brother and I dropped some more acid. I don't remember why, but the trip turned into a bummer for me. Lon seemed to be doing O.K., but I was having trouble relating to planet Earth.

I thought maybe a hamburger and a beer would bring me back to the version of reality I was familiar with – "ground" me, in other words.

We jumped into my Chevy Malibu. I fired up the little 283 engine, fumbled with the four-on-the-floor shifter, and pointed us toward the nearest café that had a beer license.

I had difficulty driving on acid. On this particular trip, it seemed I had become the *Incredible Shrinking Man*, grasping my huge steering wheel. My brother appeared to be about ten feet away in the passenger seat. His head was enormous, and I could see every pore in his face. We *must* be aliens, I thought.

Somehow, we made it safely to the café, found a booth, and ordered our hamburgers and beer. When the nice lady from Earth in her crisp white uniform, brought the burgers, I took a big juicy bite out of mine.

I experienced the whole hamburger story – and more! My years in Nebraska – the gentle cattle with their big sad eyes. The pig I saw slaughtered alive by my alcoholic uncles near Julesburg, Colorado, when I was eight-year-old. I remembered it was an unbearably hot muggy day, out on the farm. The poor pig just wouldn't die. The horrible, pitiful sounds – it all came back – magnified and amplified.

I put my hamburger down and finished my Schlitz. I ordered two more bottles of beer, chugged them, and gave up eating meat and killing animals for food or sport. Vegetarianism became my "cause" for a few days, until I remembered my reaction to the hippie girl at the love-in. I had to laugh at myself.

Chapter 16

THE DESERT

I was perched on my usual barstool, near the jukebox and within reach of the potato chip rack, at the Buccaneer Bar. It was February 1967. The Moon was full.

A little before midnight, my brother, Lon excitedly entered the bar. He told me he was in possession of a "1,000 mike" tab of acid. That's a very high dose. He suggested we go out into the desert, split the tab, and watch the sun rise. Sounded like a great idea to me! We decided Joshua Tree National Monument would be the perfect spot.

We figured it would take us about two and a half hours to get there, so we needed to get going if we wanted to be "frying" when the sun came up.

February – desert cold at night. Need jackets, blankets, big thermos hot coffee. We went to my apartment for the blankets and thermos and left Costa Mesa about one in the morning. We were driving Lon's old blue VW bus with the name and logo of his old Nebraska high school rock band, "The Panics" painted in huge letters on the sides. We called it the Panic Bus, of course.

First stop, Denny's Restaurant, to fill our thermos with hot coffee. We arrived in Joshua Tree before four in the morning. Joshua

Tree National Monument looked very spooky in the light of the full moon, that cold, quiet, February morning.

We parked the Panic Bus near a large clump of rocks several miles off the main road leading to the Monument. Lon broke the 1,000 microgram tablet of LSD into two equal portions. We washed it down with a bottle of Schlitz we brought with us from the Buccaneer, grabbed our blankets and thermos, and set out on foot into the desert. We walked aimlessly in the eerie moonlight until we came upon a large outcropping of rocks. We wanted to be settled in before sunrise. With some difficulty, we climbed to the top of the rocks and found an area where we could sit comfortably, facing the east. We each picked our individual spots, sipped hot coffee, and waited for sunrise. The full moon was at our back.

As the sun appeared on the horizon, the acid started to take effect. Five hundred micrograms was the largest dose either of us had taken. The landscape of Joshua Tree National Monument was so strange and alien to us that we might as well have been on another planet.

At first, it was wonderful, beautiful and magical. Every speck of sand sparkled like a diamond in the early morning sunlight. The desert literally came alive! We looked at each other, silently acknowledging the awe we felt in this sacred place. We began to communicate telepathically. In a split second, we understood why mystics go into the desert for spiritual experiences. We had never (in this life) thought of these matters prior to this. In that same nano second we understood the laws of karma and reincarnation. We had a simultaneous flash of us being our dad's two uncles, who worked behind the cameras in the early days of Hollywood, and who both died as young men long before Lon and I were born. We became frightened.

Lon secretly brought a portable radio with us and said out loud, "Let's hear some music!" He switched the radio on and, for the first time in my life, I heard *Strawberry Fields Forever*. It was the strangest, most in-the-now appropriate song I had ever heard. The song echoed all across the desert, and completely blew my mind! When the song ended, the "trip" changed into being scary again. The wind came up, blowing dust everywhere. We switched off the radio and found we were still communicating telepathically. We intuited that mystics and yogis struggle and perform austerities for years to have direct mystical perceptions. Through the LSD, we trespassed into this region of the mind unprepared and grossly impure. Sooner or later we would have to somehow pay our dues. We realized we might not be allowed to leave the desert. We were terrified! We knew we had to get out of there immediately, but were disoriented. Where did we park the bus? Which direction do we go to find it? Everything looked different. We had no landmarks.

We heard what sounded like childrens' voices laughing, way out in the desert. We started to follow the sound. If there were people out there, they could direct us to the road. As we walked farther into the desert, I got a bad feeling. We stopped, looked at each other, and realized there were no kids out there. It was our own minds, or the sounds of us as kids, or a desert spirit leading us away from life as we know it. We turned and ran the other way. Now the wind was really blowing. We seemed to be running in slow motion. Finally, we spotted the beautiful blue Panic Bus! Of course, the bus was breathing heavily, and the words, "The Panics" were dripping down the sides of the bus, but we knew it would get us home.

The drive back down the Twenty-Nine Palms Highway to the freeway was pretty weird. The cars we passed were all occupied by very elderly people. One guy was a skeleton dressed in a black suit. I was overcome with profound sadness and compassion. I could "read" the life story of everyone we passed: this old guy was retired military, and had done really heavy things he was ashamed of; this elderly lady was coming back from church. She had lost her faith and was filled with death anxiety. It was pretty bad. Things began to pep up again when we hit the westbound 10 Freeway. We agreed we had experienced something very profound and life-changing out there in the desert, but couldn't verbalize it. We knew we wanted more mystical experiences, but without the drugs. I knew I had to find out what "yoga" really meant.

Chapter 17

THE BIG EYE

The Joshua Tree experience had a profound impact upon me. My mind was full of thoughts of Yogis, Mystics, and Saints. When the word, "saint" came into my head, I didn't picture anything like a Catholic Saint. I thought, "A Saint is something else, but I didn't know what – maybe God in human form. Perhaps there's always been Saints on Earth. Maybe there can be more than one Saint on the Earth at the same time. Maybe we can contact these Saints. Maybe they don't perform public miracles. I don't know".

A few days later, I called in sick from my job at the machine shop. All I could think about was yogis and mystics. I found a book on the subject of spiritual aspects of yoga. The author of the book, a yogi from India, mentioned he knew of an ageless, very powerful yogi hiding in the Himalayas. The author further stated if one calls out the name of this great yogi, with sincerity and respect, that yogi will somehow make himself known. Upon reading this, I immediately called out the great yogi's name. A few minutes later there was a knock on the door. I opened the door. On my front porch was a drug dealer I barely knew. I'd seen him around the Buccaneer from time to time. He said, "This is for you", and handed me a tab of acid. He turned and walked away without another word.

I thought, "This must be the answer to my call to the great yogi in the Himalayas". I immediately forgot my post- Joshua Tree decision to seek enlightenment without drugs. I swallowed the tab, washing it down with a big glug from a cold can of Country Club Malt Liquor.

I flopped down in my big armchair, can of Country Club within reach. I remember I was wearing cut-off jeans, an orange T-shirt, and no shoes. I removed my glasses, placed them next to my malt liquor can, and closed my eyes for several minutes. Soon, I felt that funny feeling in my stomach and spine. When I opened my eyes and looked around, the walls and ceiling were breathing. The acid had come on very quickly. The trip had begun!

I saw myself as if I was partly in my body, and partly outside my body. The part of me outside my body was observing the part of me sitting in the chair.

I observed myself breaking down into my molecular structure, composed of vibrating dots of light. I saw the molecular structure of the chair vibrating at a slower rate than my body.

As my consciousness expanded, I saw not only myself and the armchair, but the apartment, street, the city of Costa Mesa, the continent, and the Earth all composed of particles of light in vibration. I saw the Earth as part of the atomic structure of the solar system.

The solar system as a component of the galaxy; all galaxies and universes as components of a greater whole.

As my consciousness expanded again, this Greater Whole took the shape of an Eye. I remember a thought flashing through my mind, "If I expand one more notch, I can see the face containing the Eye".

To my amazement, it was my own face!

I had experienced and internalized a concept I had never heard about, or as yet, read about – the microcosm and the macrocosm. The universe within and the universe without are One. We are all connected. We are *all* One!

The next day, I went back to work. I was afire with my Illumination. I ran up to grouchy old machinists shouting, "Don't you see, brother, we are all One! We must stop the war in Vietnam! We must stop killing and eating animals! We are all brothers!"

I quickly sensed from the frightened and/or disgusted way these men looked at me, they thought I was suffering brain damage from the motorcycle wreck. I made the decision right then to remain silent about mystical experiences, and just try to be one of the guys.

I wanted more, however. I wanted to be one with the universe all the time – without the LSD. I knew the acid was frying my central nervous system and producing negative side effects, but the insights I seemed to be receiving were changing my entire view of life.

Chapter 18

JUNE 1967

Prior to my LSD experiences, I wasn't much concerned with politics.

I joined the Nebraska National Guard when I was a senior in high school. Naïve patriotism and a desire to defend my country led me to join an infantry unit. Immediately after high school graduation, I was activated into the U.S. Army for Basic Training, Light Weapons Infantry Training, and something called "Basic Unit Training", which we called "bullshit under the trees!"

Upon completion of active duty, I was still required to perform four more years of Active Army Reserve and National Guard training. When I finally received my Honorable Discharge, I was bitter, angry, and cynical regarding the military and the government in general. I did not support the war in Vietnam, but didn't give it much thought, either. I had my Honorable Discharge. I fulfilled my obligation. I was out of it.

My brother, Lon, however, was an anti-war activist in high school while I was doing my Army Reserve duty. He explained why I was so angry with the Army and the government: capitalism, racism, and imperialism, of course. This all fit into the hippie bag; pot, acid, vegetarianism, Eastern philosophy, and left wing politics.

We read the *L.A. Free Press* every week for counter-culture news. In early June 1967, I noticed a small article encouraging people to attend a meeting in Los Angeles to plan a demonstration for June 23 at the Century Plaza Hotel. President Johnson was to give a speech there, so the purpose of the demonstration would be to show the President our opposition to the war in Vietnam.

Lon was most enthused! We rounded up a few Buckaroos and decided to attend the demonstration planning meeting in Los Angeles the week prior to the scheduled June twenty-third demonstration.

The day of the planning meeting, we met at the Buccaneer Bar. Our little group consisted of one angry Vietnam vet, one curious Canadian, my brother and myself. We passed around a few reefers in the parking lot of the Buccaneer, then piled into the Panic Bus. The Canadian drove. We looked like typical long-haired, bearded hippies, so we attracted the attention of the L.A.P.D. The *man* gave us a ticket for "driving too slow on the freeway". In those days, L.A.P.D. patrolled the freeways of Los Angeles. A year or two later, after a very controversial arrest and head injuries involving a beloved and harmless popular singer, the California Highway Patrol took over patrolling L.A.'s freeway system.

The demonstration planning meeting was very intense. It was loud, but well organized. It seemed to me, the leaders had the demonstration well planned before the meeting. I began to feel a little uneasy.

One incident really stands out. A now relatively well-known Hollywood writer/producer jumped up, introduced himself as a "teacher", and yelled, "The C.I.A. is in this room and I know who he is, the swine!" I cringed, and we all looked around at each other suspiciously. Years later, I saw this man's name on the credits of a movie about the assassination of JFK.

We were glad to get out of Los Angeles, and back to the Buccaneer. Lon and the other two Buckaroos decided to pass on the demonstration. I still wanted to attend, but I didn't want to go alone.

A few days prior to June 23, I noticed an announcement in the *Free Press* regarding the upcoming demonstration. A phone number was listed for further information. I called, told them I wanted to go, and asked if they could refer me to someone in the Cost Mesa area I could ride with. I was given a phone number in Irvine, California.

Ron was a professor from University of California, Irvine. He invited me to ride with his wife, Nancy, another UCI professor, Jerry G., and himself. They lived nearby, in the neighboring communities of Irvine and Laguna Beach.

I arrived at Ron and Nancy's home before noon on June twenty-third. There was to be a rally that afternoon in Los Angeles, then a march to the Century Plaza Hotel, where we would hopefully get President Johnson's attention.

On the drive from Irvine to Los Angeles, I learned Ron and Nancy were Quakers and pacifists. Jerry G was a Navy veteran. I told them I was not a pacifist, but was, like them, opposed to the war in Vietnam.

Thousands of people showed up for the rally. We read later, there were twenty thousand people! The crowd was mostly white liberals and hippies. Many families brought their children. The demonstration had been advertised as a "peaceful protest against the Vietnam War". We were told we had the necessary permits, and everything was legal. Well-known speakers gave speeches. Well-known folk singers sang folk songs. The atmosphere was very festive – and then, at dusk, the march.

As we neared the Century Plaza Hotel, the march stopped prematurely. I was in the middle of the march, so I couldn't see the front, or determine why we were stopped. We stood in place, confused, but patiently waiting for the march to continue forward. Suddenly, a convoy of busses pulled up parallel to the march. More than one thousand uniformed members of the Los Angeles Police Department emerged from the busses, and formed a line facing us.

We couldn't move forward, or go back. We were stuck in place. We tried to talk to the officers to reassure them we were peaceful. They didn't respond to us. Several minutes passed, and then they waded into us, batons swinging. They clubbed us to the ground. It was chaos. I was horrified. We got up and ran, but we seemed to be herded into dead-ends where more people were beaten bloody. Eventually, Ron, Nancy, Jerry G., and I made it back to Ron's VW bus. We rode home in shock. We were physically bruised, but psychically devastated. The only thing I remember anyone saying was, "It looked like films of Nazi Germany!"

I had, of course, seen news footage of previous civil rights and anti-war demonstrations – civil disobedience – demonstrators being carried off limply by the police. Until this night, I was under the impression the police were merely responding to non-cooperative demonstrators acting out in front of the news cameras. I hadn't seen that here. It seemed to me we were attacked brutally without provocation. On the other hand, I couldn't see the front of the march, or know what the organizers' agenda really was. All I knew was I was enraged with the police and the government. Twenty thousand white liberals and hippies may have arrived at

Century Plaza that night, but several thousand committed radicals went home.

A deep bond was formed that night between Ron, Nancy, Jerry G., and myself. We promised each other we would, from this night on, stay in continuous communication and figure out what to do next.

Ron, Nancy, and Jerry G. had never experienced mind-affecting drugs. I strongly felt, with almost religious fervor, we needed to correct that situation as soon as possible.

Chapter 19

DROPPING OUT

From early 1966 through June 1967, I worked as a chucker lathe operator for a large aerospace machine shop. We manufactured precision parts for commercial aircraft, military aircraft, and missiles.

The experience of the June twenty-third demonstration had traumatized me. Television and newspaper reports downplayed the police violence. I was there! I had witnessed passive citizens being clubbed to the ground as they attempted to comply with the police order to disperse. I would have understood if the demonstrators were resisting or even mouthing-off, and got their asses kicked by the cops. We were sincerely attempting to do what they ordered us to do.

My co-workers at the factory, and even some of the Buckaroos, either didn't believe me, or thought I was exaggerating. It was driving me nuts!

I decided I was through participating in anything that supported the Vietnam War. At the factory, the parts we manufactured were easy to identify. If I received a blueprint stamped "Redstone Arsenal" I could be sure it was for the military.

The Monday following the demonstration, I showed up at work. Sure enough, a blueprint marked "Redstone Arsenal" was on my workbench. I called my leadman over, and told him I wasn't working on military jobs anymore. I reminded him we had plenty of commercial work he could give me. He walked away with no comment. Five minutes later, the leadman, the foreman, the production manager, and a vice president were gathered around my machine. I repeated what I told my leadman. The foreman said, "You'll work on whatever we give you. You can't pick and choose your jobs". I knew he was probably correct legally, but I didn't care at that point.

I replied with some kind of semi-incoherent, self-righteous anti-war, anti-imperialism speech.

The production manager told me I was fired. "Clean out any company property from your toolbox. You'll never work in this industry again".

I cleaned out my toolbox. A security guard inspected it and helped me load it into the trunk of my car. I went back into the shop to pick up my final check, and yelled, "Capitalist warmongers!" as I sprinted to my car. I sped away, burning rubber through the parking lot.

Back at the Buccaneer, nobody was sympathetic to my whining. In fact, Jack, the owner of the Buccaneer, called me a "commie pinko" and told me I should "complain to the chaplain, or Fie-dell Castro, or someone who gives a shit. In fact, why don't you go back to Roo'-sha or Red China, or wherever the hell you come from!"

I had to laugh, even though I felt depressed and isolated. "I'm from Long Beach, Jack".

Chapter 20

HITCHHIKING TO SAN FRANCISCO

July Fourth, 1967 was my own little Independence Day. I left my significant other and our duplex apartment in Costa Mesa. I was off to "find myself". This was the famous Summer of Love, and hippies, runaways, drifters, and the curious were flooding into San Francisco, with "flowers in their hair". I didn't have flowers in my hair. I was wearing Levis, steel-toed combat boots with an ankle bell, a colorful T-shirt, and an East Indian necklace. I also carried a large, very sharp folding knife in my pocket. An extra pair of Levis, my old Army field jacket, socks, and T-shirts were neatly packed in an AWOL bag. I agonized over whether to bring a sleeping bag, or just travel light and free. Light and free won out. Oh, yes, I carried a soft cover book on Hinduism, which I hadn't yet attempted to read.

My destination was Haight-Ashbury. I thought, "I'll just walk down Newport Boulevard to Pacific Coast Highway early this morning, stick out my thumb, and I'll be in San Francisco with the hippies tonight! Let's see... about four hundred and fifty miles at fifty miles per hour...nine hours, plus refreshment stops, of course.

It took two full days to hitch from Costa Mesa to San Francisco. I became stranded near Lompoc in the middle of the night. The few passing cars contained military personnel from Vandenberg Air Force Base. They yelled "hippie freak" or "draft dodger" at me. I felt very vulnerable out there, and pissed off. I was nearly twenty-five years old, and had an Honorable Discharge from the U.S. Army. How dare they call me a "draft dodger"? "Hippie freak", I could live with.

I finally got a ride with a very creepy guy who was going to San Jose. I decided I would ride with him to San Jose, and take a bus into San Francisco. The adventure of hitchhiking had worn very thin.

We passed through Santa Maria about midnight. It was very foggy on Highway 101, and we never exceeded forty miles per hour. The driver was a huge hulk of a guy. He said he was from Las Vegas, and knew Frank Sinatra really well. He told me creepy, scary things about Mr. Sinatra. I didn't want to hear them, and secretly had my hand on my knife the entire way to San Jose.

Upon arrival in San Jose, I boarded the first available bus to San Francisco. On the bus, I pretended to read my book on Hinduism. I thought I would look like a deep-thinker and truth-seeker.

Two hours later, I was in downtown San Francisco. It was a hot July day, and the walk to Market and Haight already had me sweating. The walk to Haight and Ashbury was a very long uphill trek.

I ducked into a bar on Haight to take a beer break. From the tone of the barroom conversations, it was obvious the alcoholics of San Francisco didn't care for the hippies. I didn't feel very welcome, so I chugged my beer and left.

As I finally neared Ashbury Street, I encountered a man about my age. He extended his hand to me and said, "Welcome to San Francisco, Marc". I was taken aback, but thought perhaps we knew each other from Southern California. I asked, "Do I know you?" He replied, "My brother and I did some acid and we saw you in the cloud formations. You and your brother did acid at the same time". Now, I was getting kind of freaked out. He must have introduced himself, but I don't remember, I was so thrown off-balance by all this.

He walked up Haight Street with me, pointing out places to crash, cheap cafes, little markets – "They're Chinese Communists, but they're O.K.", and a hippie-friendly laundromat. He explained one side of Haight Street was still "pure", but the other side was corrupted by "the Mafia". The Mafia side of the street had been flooded with speed. He said, "speedfreaks have ruined the Haight", and there had been several drug-related murders already that summer. My strange tour guide paused, tranced-out a few seconds, and told me he had to go to his apartment immediately. His wife was "messing around", and he had to " throw her out the window". I never saw him again.

I hung around the Haight for a week or so, talking to other hippies. A recurring theme I heard was "the real hippies are leaving the City and going to Big Sur to form communes in the forest".

I left San Francisco, and started hitching my way south on Highway 1. A carload of Mexican-Americans picked me up just south of San Francisco. They told me the car wasn't really theirs, and when it ran out of gas, they would abandon it and hitch to Los Angeles.

We ran out of gas at Big Sur late that night. They left the car on the shoulder of the highway. The last I saw of them, as I headed into the forest, was the group of them standing along the deserted highway with their thumbs out.

I found a little clearing in the forest, and covered myself up with my old Army field jacket and tried to sleep.

ORANGE SUNSHINE

The following morning, I ran into several hippies, who shared their peanut butter sandwiches with me. They told me they were joining an extremely isolated commune on top of a mountain deep in the forest. With some reservation, I joined them. We hiked and climbed, and climbed, and climbed. I was hot, out-of -breath, thirsty, and was beginning to tire of the wonder and beauty of nature. I told the others I was going back down to Big Sur. They said it was only a couple more miles, but I just wanted to see the highway again, so I cut out.

I bought a six-pack of beer at the Big Sur general store, chugged it, peed in a real toilet, and washed my hands in a real sink. Civilization is good! I walked over to Highway 1, stuck out my thumb, and continued south.

My first ride was with a lady who had very long pure-white hair. As I got into the car, I noticed she had bells attached to leather wrist and ankle straps on the backseat. She told me I "belonged" in Big Sur, and should stay and enjoy the rituals they held in the forest. Once again, I got that nervous feeling. I told her I needed to get back to L.A. –"family difficulties". She said, "That's unfortunate", stopped the car, and let me out to continue my southbound trek.

The next ride was the stereotypical VW hippie bus. My hosts were a very nice, well educated, but extremely codependent couple about my age. Twenty-five seemed very mature in the hippie alternate reality of 1967.

Along with myself, there were four other passengers; two white guys, an African-American girl, and a white girl. They appeared to be between eighteen and twenty-two, and were all smoking pot non-stop. An interesting note is, during this entire San Francisco/Big Sur road trip, I hadn't used any drugs other than alcohol. The psychos and psychics I met were trippy enough for me!

When I climbed into the bus, the driver informed me they were headed to Los Angeles, and suggested I might like the Venice Beach area. I expressed gratitude and said, "Venice sounds good to me".

I kept to myself in the back of the bus, very turned-off by the behavior of my fellow passengers. All they did was take. They ate all our hosts' food; they smoked all our hosts' dope, and they offered nothing in return. One of the guys tried to hit on the young black woman by saying, "I really dig spade chicks". She didn't seem offended!

I didn't like these parasites. Where was the love and the sharing I associated with being a "hippie"? The couple who owned the bus were very loving, but they had no boundaries. I felt sorry for them.

Big Sur to Venice is a long ride down Highway 1. Several times we stopped for beer and sandwiches. It was obvious everyone had some money on them. When we arrived at Venice Beach, however, I was the only one who offered a few buck for gas, and actually said, "Thank you". At that moment I felt like a grouchy Republican hippie! I was ashamed I even looked like these freeloading narcissists.

Venice Beach somewhat restored my faith in the hippie movement. I connected to many people who were really trying to live the life – working a little, sharing appropriately, being considerate of others – yet not taking shit from anyone.

I stayed with several groups of good people, living in mini-urban communes in the Venice Beach area. That fall, I drifted south to Costa Mesa. I wanted to tell Ron, Nancy, and all the Buckaroos about my Summer of Love adventures.

Chapter 21

HIGH TAILIN' IT TO OREGON

San Francisco's Summer of Love was a little too weird for me, and I returned to my little duplex apartment in Costa Mesa in the fall of 1967.

I became more interested in yoga, and tried to combine LSD and yoga philosophy. In those days, there weren't many books available on yoga. I didn't have a teacher, of course, so I began practicing a series of Hatha Yoga postures. I learned these *asanas* from a small book by a very popular-with-the-Beatles yogi from India. I tried to assume the postures described in this little illustrated booklet. My body soon became more flexible and healthy, and my ego became unmanageable. I studied Hatha Yoga, Raja Yoga, Giani Yoga, and Bhakti Yogi from a series of books written in 1904. I thought reading these books while I was frying on high doses of LSD was the same thing as mastering the yoga.

I read *Autobiography of a Yogi*, by Paramahansa Yogananda, and joined Self-Realization Fellowship. I started taking their lessons by mail, and practicing the beginning stages of the SRF meditation. I arrogantly and disrespectfully assumed they wouldn't mind if I enhanced my meditation with acid, pot, or hash. Lon and I attended an eight-hour group meditation stoned on my homemade brownies.

The monks of the Self Realization Fellowship glared at us disapprovingly.

I quietly and humbly proclaimed to myself that I was probably a guru. I preached to Ron, Nancy and others about the nature of reality. I actually walked around Costa Mesa wearing sandals and carrying a staff for a day or two. I received a little too much attention from the citizens, so I figured I'd do better undercover, impersonating a regular human being.

I reported to our little group of truth seekers what I'd heard in San Francisco – that people were leaving the cities and forming rural communes. Ron and Nancy were excited by the idea. They told me they knew a healer in southern Oregon who wanted to sell some of his river front property on the edge of the Siskiyou National Forest. His vision was to sell the property to "good people", not developers. We eventually pooled our money and bought some land!

Martin Luther King was assassinated on April fourth, 1968. I was at Ron and Nancy's home in Irvine. We were watching the news. Cities were burning. People were afraid, angry, and confused. We believed it was now time for us to leave Southern California and begin our new life of peace, love, brotherhood, and extreme poverty in rural Oregon. We left for Oregon ten days after the King assassination.

Our little Orange County group had grown considerably by the time we departed for Oregon. Nearly thirty people from Costa Mesa, Laguna Beach, and University of California, Irvine decided to move to an area none of us had ever seen!

We set out in a convoy of VW buses and U-Haul trucks. More people from the San Francisco Bay area joined us up there.

In political correctspeak, we "celebrated diversity". Our new community included two university professors, an attorney, a professional folk singer, a concert violinist, blue collar factory workers, a carpenter, a con-man, a yoga instructor, and two former strippers.

We were white, African-American, and Native-American. We were Protestants, Roman Catholics, Jews, and one Hare Krishna monk.

We were heterosexuals, lesbians, gays and bisexuals. Several folks were undecided. We were alcoholics, drug addicts, recovering alcoholic/addicts, celibates, and practicing sexual addicts.

We were single people, married couples, and families with kids. We were vegetarians and meat-eaters.

We were the vanguard of the Age of Aquarius. We were the wave of the future. We had no unifying philosophy or political point-of-view. We were just going to love everyone, and everyone was going to love us.

Upon arriving in Oregon, we bought our land and settled along the Illinois River, near the California-Oregon border. Our plan was to build little single-family houses using communal labor, like they did in the pioneer days. We would have a big communal garden, and the friendly local people would teach us "how to do stuff".

We did not know our beautiful valley was already occupied by survivalists and white power advocates who had moved in several years previously. We soon found out.

Even most of the old time local residents were hostile to us. They thought we were drug-crazed communists. Come to think of it, in a way they were right.

We thought we could win them over eventually, but being stoned all the time, we really didn't have a clear picture of our situation.

Chapter 22

READ YER CARDS, BROTHER?

Our little group of Orange County hippies became generally known as the "Takilma Road People". We were a relatively conservative lot, compared with some of the other communes along the West Coast. We advocated serial monogamy and family unity. We tried to be as honest as we could be in our dealings with other people, and we didn't shoot drugs into our veins. Several of our group were celibate and drug free.

In the summer of 1968, several other communes sprang up in southern Oregon. Many of them called themselves "Families".

The nearest commune to us was called the Fanatic Family. From what I understood at the time, the Fanatic Family was a loose-knit group of communes. They had an urban commune in the San Francisco/Oakland area. Their rural commune in our area was about five miles from us. Some of their group would drop in on us from time to time. They were very "speedy", but funny and likable. I was always happy to see them come by, and just as happy to see them leave.

The Family of the Mystic Arts appeared in the Medford area in late 1968. They were really "into nature", and I thought they were creepy. Several of our group left Takilma and joined them in their commune deep in the forest.

Several smaller "Families" took over mining claims in the area and attempted to live on them rent free.

Although we had no unifying philosophy, most of us shared some common beliefs. We believed two cosmic events were happening simultaneously: The Creation, as a whole, was descending into Kal Yuga, the darkest age in the Hindu timetable. Civilization was degenerating. On the other hand, many of us also believed we were entering the Age of Aquarius. This new age would arise from the ashes of the old. We were part of this New Age. Some of us were convinced catastrophic geological changes were imminent, and we had been "called" to leave the cities and settle into these geological safe areas near the Oregon Vortex.

Located near Gold Hill, Oregon, not far from Grants Pass, the Oregon Vortex is a very unusual place. The Vortex is a spherical field of force, half above the ground –half below. It has a diameter of about two hundred feet. Within that diameter, light and gravity seem to be "different". The Vortex was a tourist attraction, and had a gift shop run by an apparently knowledgeable man. He seemed to know many interesting stories concerning the Vortex. He told us the Oregon Vortex was a powerful force field, so powerful that the speed of light actually slowed down passing through it. He said the Native American Indians called it "the forbidden ground" .Who had called us, psychically and telepathically, to leave Orange County and settle here near the Vortex? Well, the Space Brothers, of course! We believed in UFOs. We saw unexplained lights in the sky almost any night we wanted to look. It didn't matter if we were stoned or not. There was most unusual activity in the sky near the Oregon Vortex. Sometimes these lights would appear in a triangular formation.

We all had different theories about the UFOs and the Space Brothers. Some of us thought they were angelic beings, much more evolved than us. Some of us thought they were demonic mind-fuckers. I alternated between these two polarities of thought.

An experience regarding one Family's concept of the UFOs really stands out. One hot July day, Lon and I were clearing brush around our camp on Takilma Road. An old pickup truck pulled off the road, and into our camp. I was coming off some acid I'd taken the previous night, so I was very sensitive to say the least!

Three long-haired scraggly bearded men and a thin hard-looking woman occupied the truck. One of the men was sitting in the open bed of the pickup, holding a Winchester Model 94, 30-30 rifle. He remained in that position. I observed an open case of beer in the pickup bed as well. The other two guys and the woman got out of the cab and walked over to Lon and I. They were all wearing hunting knives in leather sheaths.

The apparent leader strode up to Lon and I, stuck out his hand, gave us the Brotherhood Handshake, and introduced himself. I don't remember his name, so I'll call him "Dirk". He told us they were up from Oakland and were camped on a mining claim up in the hills, about ten miles from Takilma. Dirk said they'd heard of our group and were delivering a message from the Space Brothers: A Mother Ship was hovering over their mining claim, waiting to beam us all aboard. The Aliens would then transport us to our new home, as this planet was on the verge of a "polar shift". The ship was operating at such a high vibratory rate it couldn't be seen with our human physical eyes. In fact, we wouldn't be able to beam up in our physical bodies. We would have to leave our physical bodies behind, and beam up in our astral, mental, and spiritual bodies. Dirk and his Family's mission was to invite us to their mining claim, give us a big dinner of venison steaks, mescaline and beer, and then help us out of our physical bodies.

Lon and I nervously told Dirk we were vegetarians. Dirk told us it would be "O.K. to eat meat one last time. Enjoy yourselves!"

We told Dirk we followed another spiritual path and needed to remain on Earth for the polar shift – for "karmic reasons". Dirk said, "O.K., it's your loss", and pulled out a Tarot card deck from a leather medicine bag. He asked, in a voice from the grave, "Read yer cards, brother?" Such evil radiating off ol' Dirk – it was awful! We refused politely, and they left.

Looking back, the feeling I got from being around Dirk and his crew was they were similar to an infamous Family in Los Angeles, operating at about the same time.

They had their own version of reality that they must have agreed upon, drugs and alcohol reinforced it, and the leader was a homicidal psychopath.

Chapter 23

NORTH-SOUTH

Takilma Road was a narrow gravel road that branched off a paved road leading to Cave Junction, Oregon, eight miles to the north.

Southbound, Takilma Road ran parallel to the Illinois River and dead-ended in the Siskiyou National Forest – probably on the California side of the Oregon/California border. In other words, anyone driving south on Takilma Road, passing our hippie camps, would have to turn around eventually and head back north on the same road. There was no other way.

Many unusual people appeared on Takilma Road in 1968

Early one morning I emerged from my tent, carrying a snake that my cat, Spooky, had presented me as a trophy. "No, Spooky, we are vegetarians". Setting the snake free, I glanced through the forest and spotted a wild man standing in the middle of Takilma Road. He was facing South, holding up a cardboard sign that said, "NORTH'. I went over to find out what *his* trip was.

He introduced himself as "Saul", and we shook hands. His handshake was most unusual. He faced me squarely, grabbed my right hand with his right hand, and my left hand with his left hand. Our arms formed an "X". He looked me directly in the eyes and shook both of our arms three distinct "shakes". It was a little like

76

shaking hands with a dynamo. Every member of our little group straggled out to meet and shake hands with Saul.

Saul was a man of few words, but had very clean, pure energy. We asked him to stay for dinner and invited him to crash at our camp. He told us he was a vegetarian. We said we were, too. He stayed for dinner.

We had vegetarian tacos, but one of the ingredients contained egg whites. We didn't care. I don't know why we thought an egg was a vegetable or a dairy product. We just didn't think that deeply about such things.

After he had eaten, Saul became sick. He asked if there were eggs in his food. We lied and said we didn't know for sure. He was pissed of and really ill.

Saul went out into the forest to sleep it off. We all felt really bad. Early the next morning, I saw Saul standing in the middle of Takilma Road. He was facing north, holding up a big cardboard sign that said, "SOUTH".

Chapter 24

GHOST STORIES

Most long-time residents of the Cave Junction area were opposed to our hippie philosophy and our use of drugs other than alcohol.

A few neighbors, however, were friendly and supportive. One such family lived less than a mile down Takilma Road from us. They were Native Americans. They lived in a house, had a TV, drank beer, and baked delicious homemade bread.

Twice a month I'd bring over a case of beer and watch TV with this cozy little family. We'd sit on a big soft couch and eat homemade bread made from the Government food commodities we all received once a month. Even the tons of butter we'd pile on our bread came from the *man*, who gave us food instead of food stamps.

It seemed like about every two weeks I'd get so fed up living in Nature I couldn't stand to look at another tree! That's when I would walk over to the Decker's house, so I could actually sit on a couch in front of a TV. Sixteen ounce cans of beer in hand, we'd all talk shit and laugh at ourselves.

I felt safe with this Native American family. They were very open to talking about sacred power places, UFOs, and related subjects. This *was* 1968, and most normal families thought these things were too "kooky" to speak seriously about.

The Decker family had lived in the Illinois Valley of southern Oregon all their lives. They told me they had seen UFOs so many times they were unimpressed with even the most dramatic sightings. They re-affirmed what I'd already been told; the largest, most well-known and most studied "sacred power place" in the area was the Oregon Vortex, located in the Gold Hill area near Grants Pass.

Our neighbors also said there were other power spots nearby that were unknown to the public. They told me of very powerful vortices deep in the Siskiyou National Forest. There were stories of prospectors being knocked to their knees by the energy; circular areas bare of trees; and trees around the circumference of these areas growing out at an angle instead of perpendicular to the ground. They said these areas, and the Oregon Vortex, were traditionally known to the Native Americans as "sacred spots".

One of the stories this family told me really gave me the chills. The dad stated that late one night, several months before we moved up there, they saw a real ghost. The family was sitting around, watching TV. They heard a horse ride up Takilma Road and onto their dirt and gravel driveway. A few moments later there was a loud knock on the door. Several of the adult family members went to the door, opened it, and saw a wild-eyed cowboy standing before them. He was dressed in authentic-looking late 19th century cowboy clothes. The cowboy told them he'd just been shot in a saloon and now didn't know where he was. The family was speechless. In his confused state, the cowboy turned, got back on his horse, and rode off into the night.

I believed the story, and I believed just about any kind of freaky experience could manifest on or near Takilma Road. The longer I lived there, the more I wanted to leave.

I longed to see concrete, oil refineries, gangsta graffiti, freeways and gridlock. I longed to hear the lullaby of police sirens in the night! I would actually say things like, "Too much nature ain't healthy for a guy!" and, "If you've seen one tree, you've seen 'em all!" My tree-hugging hippie brothers and sisters looked at me aghast. That's why I'd say it -- just to mess with 'em.

Chapter 25

SPACESHIP EARTH

Insanity or death held no great terror for me in my Takilma hippie days. Prior to moving to Oregon I had an LSD experience so terrifying I thought I would have to be taken to the mental hospital. As my mind was melting down, I thought, with the tiny fraction of my mind that could think in words, "I'll just try to be helpful to the other patients with whatever capabilities I have remaining". I visualized myself tying another patient's shoelaces. Immediately I was restored to sanity, or at least normal baseline consciousness. Later, I realized mental patients probably don't have shoelaces.

Regarding death, I thought a dramatic Christ-like end would be appropriate. Nothing too painful or disfiguring, though. Just deep meaningful looks, and tearful loved ones. "Yes, he really was not of this Earth. Look, a comet!"

I didn't want to die at the hands of Dirk and his "family", or be killed by some drunken redneck, but those were distinct possibilities in that space/time location.

My brother, Lon and I discouraged Dirk and his plan to relieve us of our physical bodies, so we could beam up to the Mother Ship. The local rednecks, however, were another story. They were violently opposed to us and wouldn't go away. We'd build a cabin or other structure -- they'd burn it down at night. The situation became so hostile, I secretly armed myself.

One Sunday afternoon, a carload of locals pointed the muzzle of a rifle out their car window and fired at us as they drove past our home site. The idiots had small children in the car, so we couldn't return fire. We had to hit the dirt and crawl to cover.

The worst thing that happened while I was in Takilma was the beating of Gary, the gentle, kind man who sold us our land. One night, five carloads of locals descended upon Gary and Diane's farmhouse. They blocked the two entrances to his yard and called him out. When he came out of his house, unarmed, they beat him with tire irons. Diane, Gary's wife, told us later, "He just kept repeating 'Jesus loves you' to the cowardly assholes as they beat him". Gary was hospitalized with broken bones, cuts, and lots of bruises.

That did it for me. From then on, I never went anywhere without my nine millimeter German P-38 pistol. I took a small group of us to a gun store in Grants Pass, where we purchased more firearms and ammo. I gave basic firearm safety and shooting lessons in the riverbed behind our camp. My students were any not-too-stoned hippies who believed in self-defense. Soon, our Takilma group polarized into two factions: The "OM-ers", and the "Shooters". We even laughed about it and more-or-less respected each other's position.

Whenever I took LSD (or peyote, or mescaline, or STP), I put my pistol away and entered other regions.

At sunrise, one beautiful fall morning, I dropped two tabs of purple Owsley acid and ventured into the forest alone. This wasn't quite as foolhardy as it may seem. I just followed the river into the forest, and south toward the unmarked California border. I felt safe near the river. I felt unsafe if I wasn't within sight of the river. Deeper into the forest, it got downright creepy. I felt a presence in the forest; a very ancient conscious *presence* –not benevolent. I didn't feel it near the river.

After a few hours of hiking along the river, I sat down to rest and observe. In my altered state, I was made aware of how the entire forest was interconnected. I noticed the roots of the trees clinging to the riverbank, and could actually "see" the roots taking water and nutrients from the ground. Everything depended upon, and was a part of, everything else; yet it looked somehow artificial.

Then, I heard the Sound! A deep HUM coming from within the earth – like the sound of a gigantic engine. I could feel the vibration.

I thought, "Maybe we're on an enormous spaceship. The forest, the soil, the river - nature itself – is artificial, yet conscious".

We don't have a clue how we got here, who we really are, where we came from, or where we're headed.

It's real, yet it's all an illusion. It's fake, but we're not supposed to notice. I decided I wouldn't talk about this experience when I returned to the commune. What would be the point?

Chapter 26

TWO PRIESTS

Mr. Dupre was another one of our neighbors on Takilma Road. He was a rancher, and a lifelong resident of the area. Mr. Dupre had a reputation for being quite a character. He was a real cowboy. He patrolled his large ranch on horseback, a single-action Army .45 Long Colt on his hip, and a snootful of whisky on his breath. His voice was gruff and gravelly.

Mr. Dupre tolerated us hippies. He admired our independence and our desire to distance ourselves from the *man*. We liked Mr. Dupre, but were scared of him as well. He was a racist, an alcoholic, and he brandished that .45 Colt revolver a little too indiscriminately.

One morning, Mr. Dupre rode over to our camp on Takilma Road. He was on horseback, followed by his two big mean dogs, Trigger and Nigger.

He wanted to make a deal with us. We all needed a large quantity of firewood to see us through the winter. Mr. Dupre cut down a number of trees on his ranch and had dragged the felled trees into his meadow. He set up a large circular saw near the stack of felled trees.

We were to cut all the trees into firewood-sized logs. In return for our labor, we could keep half the logs for our own winter supply.

Twelve of our Takilma group drove out into Mr. Dupre's meadow, in our VW buses for a fun day of sawing.

It was a beautiful, crisp, cool fall day, and we were actually having fun. Some of us were smoking pot. I wasn't, because at this point I considered myself a yogi and a mystic. Marijuana stimulates the lower chakras. LSD and mescaline were *my* sacraments. I believed they activated the higher chakras – the heart, the throat, the third-eye, and the crown. I secretly looked down on potheads, but tried not to show my disdain. They were doing the best they could according to their light!

Several hours into our work, we noticed a black Mercedes-Benz sedan bumping through the meadow. It was headed our way. Mr. Dupre's two dogs were running behind the Mercedes, barking like crazy. The black sedan pulled up next to our hippie sawmill operation. Two Roman Catholic priests got out of the car. They were dressed in black traditional priestly garb. Mr. Dupre's dogs continued to bark wildly, as if they knew the two priests. The older, grouchier-looking priest shouted angrily at the dogs, "Down, Trigger! Down, Nigger!"

We were shocked to hear the "N" word shouted like that – from a priest, yet. The whole scene was so surreal. The black Mercedes-Benz, driving off the road in the middle of a meadow surrounded by thick forests; the two priests, looking so medieval; our hippie sawmill; us hard-core hippies, who had been living in the woods for about six months without housing, showers, or toilets. The contrast was exquisite.

When the dogs finally settled down, the younger priest explained they had "come out here to check-up on a young woman in this commune". They identified the woman, who was with us. The priest told her that her parents, in the Midwest, had become concerned she had joined a cult out here in the Oregon woods.

The woman came forward to reassure the priest she was healthy, happy, and was with our group of her own free will. We all unconsciously formed a protective circle around our Takilma sister, just in case the priests were there to snatch her and attempt to return her to her family. She was over eighteen, married, and *was* happy in Takilma. We assumed a very defensive attitude and posture just in case.

We *looked* like a damn cult! Forming a circle around the young woman and the priests; not letting the priests talk to her alone. Two of our group – a tall eastern European named Gipsy Dan, and a one-armed former pachuco-turned-yogi, known to us only as "Duke", hassled the priests aggressively. They confronted the priests about the Church's history of, "taking the gold, and leaving the peasants in the dirt", the Inquisition, and the question of "Where was the Church during the holocaust?"

We certainly were a self-righteous bunch, for all our preaching about unconditional love.

The situation here was simple. Connie's parents in the Midwest were worried. They called their parish priests. Those priests called the Church in Grants Pass, who sent these jokers, who obviously knew Mr. Dupre and his dogs. No big deal.

The priests reported back to Connie's parents that she was healthy and seemed happy, but was part of a somewhat disorganized hippie commune. Her parents then called the local Sheriff, and he hassled us for a few weeks. On one occasion, the Sheriff drove out to Lon's cabin to question him regarding Connie's parents' concerns. Lon was having his "day of silence" and wrote a note to the Sheriff asking him to return another day, as he could not "break his silence". The Sheriff was enraged. He stormed out to his car, slammed the car door, and sped off throwing gravel a quarter of a mile!

Chapter 27

CUCUMBER FIELDS FOREVER

By late fall, 1968, my little cabin on Takilma Road was just beginning to take form.

We built a good solid foundation. The frame was erected and the outside walls were nailed on. We were almost finished with the roof. Of course there were no plans for running water or electricity. We had a well nearby and there was always the Illinois River for our daily baths. I pretended it was the Ganges.

I had built a very sturdy outhouse, but it had been condemned by the County Inspectors. The *man* didn't want us there and was not subtle about it. When we went to Grants Pass to obtain our Oregon Driver's Licenses, the DMV refused to let us pass our driving tests. Hippies who drove up to Portland reported they had no trouble obtaining Oregon licenses in that cosmopolitan city. When any of us Takilma hippies built a suitable outhouse or other structure, it would be condemned by the County Inspectors. This was not paranoia on our part; it was a well-organized effort to get us out of southern Oregon.

We knew very soon that the weather would turn really cold and rainy. I wanted to be able to sleep indoors before fall turned to winter. We *were* bathing in the river and "going to the bathroom" in the woods.

I moved a wood stove into the uncompleted cabin, where the kitchen was to be, and brought sleeping bags up into the soon-to-be cozy sleeping loft.

I needed windows, but was running out of money. I had enough lumber to finish the cabin already stacked outside and paid for.

Most of our little Takilma group was in a similar financial condition. We had to get some money, so we decided to look for temporary work.

We told our Native American neighbors about our financial plight. They suggested we do what the locals do when they need a little extra money – agricultural day labor. They told us where to show up and at six the next morning, the Takilma hippies began our short-lived farm worker careers.

Our job was to pick rotten cucumbers off the ground and put them into five-gallon buckets, which we carried – one in each hand. We were to fill the buckets with cucumbers and empty the buckets into a machine pulled by a tractor. The machine's job was to extract the seeds from the rotten cucumbers, keep the seeds, and deposit the remains onto the ground.

It looked easy, watching the local workers, mostly women, do it. They talked, gossiped, and laughed as they worked. Some were senior citizens, one was slightly disabled, and one girl was more than eight months pregnant. The other women joked about having to deliver the baby in the cucumber field.

Our average age was twenty-five. Most of us did Hatha Yoga every day and thought we were in pretty good condition. We couldn't begin to keep up with these local out-of-shape women. We fell down. We complained loudly. We couldn't keep up with the tractor. We repeatedly dropped our buckets and spilled our cucumbers.

Somehow, we finished this hellish day and got paid. The local women weren't even tired. They wanted to do another field! We barely were able to drag ourselves back to Takilma Road.

The following morning, I took the Panic Bus and my cucumber-picking money, and drove the sixty miles to Grants Pass, the nearest big town. On the outskirts of Grants Pass there were big stores that sold used household articles and supplies- sort of a cross between Home Depot and the Goodwill, without the good will.

I found just the windows and frames I needed, paid for them with my cucumber-picking money, and loaded them carefully into the Panic Bus.

My back was sore from bending over all day in the cucumber field, and my arms were aching from carrying the heavy buckets at odd angles, but on the drive back from Grants Pass, I was feeling good. I had my windows and frames, and was going to be warm and dry when we finished the roof and installed the windows.

In my rare moment of happiness, I took a corner too fast. The windows fell from where I had placed them in the back of the bus. Every window shattered. Broken glass scattered all over the floor of the bus.

I drove straight to the unofficial Takilma Dump and silently unloaded the now empty window frames and all the broken glass.

My next stop was a liquor store in Cave Junction, eight miles from Takilma. Inside the liquor store, I fantasized what I would do if some redneck messed with me in my present mood. I was prepared to blast him into his next incarnation with my "nine". At that point in the day, I truly didn't give a shit. I purchased two six packs of

Country Club Malt Liquor and a huge bag of salted peanuts in the shells, and drove miles into the forest on an old logging road.

I parked the Panic Bus, drank all the malt liquor, ate all the peanuts, and wept uncontrollably for about fifteen minutes. I pitched the empty cans into the woods, brushed the peanut shells out the door, blew my nose and wiped my eyes.

I headed back to my never-to-be-finished home on Takilma Road.

Chapter 28

THE RIVER OF TIME

Winter was almost upon us. My little cabin was still only about two-thirds completed. The roof was finished, but there were big open spaces in the walls where the window frames and windows were supposed to be. The wood stove was in the kitchen area, and the sleeping loft was completed. The inside of the cabin was one open, rectangular space. I had no furniture, so it looked and felt pretty roomy.

Our Takilma group was hosting three long-haired, bearded men from the Berkeley/Oakland area. They were quiet, serious guys in their late twenties or early thirties. They seemed like hippies on the outside, and soldiers on the inside. They only stayed a few days, but they left us a small stash of LSD tablets.

On their last day in Takilma, the three strangers, two of the Takilma men, and myself, took the LSD and "tripped out" in my cabin. We sat on cushions scattered around the cabin floor. I sat in a half-lotus, with my back against the wall. We all remained silent, and just went inside ourselves.

At one point, I looked around at the other men and *knew* we had all been together many times in the past.

The inside of the cabin changed. It was the old west. We looked like cowboys. I was an outlaw preacher, and the other men were part of the gang I traveled with. The three guys from the Bay Area looked at me knowingly, as if they were on the same wave length. Suddenly, I felt fear -- not of the men in the cabin, but of the posse who was coming for us. The scene shifted.

We were in ancient China. We were highly successful and very prosperous river pirates. I had no idea why I knew we were river pirates, because in that incarnation we looked like royalty. We were wearing robes bearing the symbol of the dragon. I was feeling very smug because I had just completed a bloodless interrogation of someone, and had extracted the information we were seeking for our next mission (robbery?). The scene shifted again.

We appeared to be in the distant future, still in the woods, but not on this Earth. In the background I could hear electronic chatter. We looked like our 1968 selves, but with computer implants installed in our bodies. I could actually "see" our ganglia and nervous systems. My mood was calm and detached. I could understand the exterior electronic noise, and communicate telepathically with the other men in the room. Once again, we seemed to be experiencing the same thing. In this futuristic or parallel reality world, we were to be on some sort of exploration, or geological mission. My 1968 and current states of consciousness are clueless as to what we were doing in that future or parallel life.

The final scene appeared to be the immediate future. The room was empty and I was afraid. It was dark. Vigilantes were outside. They were burning us out. I could hear them cursing and yelling at us as they torched our cabins. People were running through the forest. All was panic and chaos. The vision ended.

I was back in my cabin with the guys. It was present time. One of the Bay Area men looked at me. "What the hell was going on with that last one?" I told him I didn't know, but it appeared the locals weren't content to beat up the guy who sold us our land; they wanted us out completely.

I felt great anxiety, and a tremendous sense of urgency to get out of southern Oregon!

Chapter 29

HIGHTAILIN' IT BACK HOME

My vision of our Takilma group being burned out by night riders really had me disturbed. I was still coming off the acid trip that had induced the visions, so the scenes and associated emotions were still very clear.

Even the logical part of my mind knew this was a very likely scenario. I mentally recounted our past run-ins with the natives.

We were denied Oregon Driver's Licenses from the local DMV. Hippies who traveled to Portland had no problems obtaining new licenses.

Our up-to-code outhouses were condemned as soon as they were constructed. We were thus required to "shit in the woods", or find a friendly neighbor who would let us use their facilities.

One beautiful just-completed cabin, constructed in the shape of a pyramid, had been burned to the ground by vigilantes.

An African-American member of our group had a dog "sic'd" on him by a local racist as he walked along a nearby country road.

We'd been denied service in the nearby town. One of our group reported he'd seen a sign in a store window, "NO NIGGERS OR HIPPIES ALLOWED".

The man who sold us our land had been severely beaten by a gang of local night riders. He was hospitalized for weeks due to his injuries. We had been shot at.

A local law enforcement officer actually told us he sided with those who opposed us. He stated he was ex-military intelligence, and he "knew what we were up to".

We certainly didn't know what we were up to – not consciously, at least. My feeling was we were pawns in some kind of multi-dimensional psycho- social experiment. I didn't know, or care, who our puppet masters were, but for me the experiment was over. I wanted out – now!

I told my brother we had to leave Takilma immediately. The entire Takilma hippie community was in danger if *we* didn't leave right now. Somehow, Lon and I were a focal point for the negativity aligned against us. This was on a psychic, or energetic level, because in the physical world, we weren't treated any worse than the other hippies. We didn't even stand out that much.

Lon didn't hesitate. We packed up the blue Panic Bus that night. We told our Takilma neighbors what we were doing. They didn't understand, but being hippies, cheerfully replied, "Whatever, man". Our hippie neighbors agreed to keep an eye on our property and unfinished cabins until we returned.

The two- day drive back to Southern California was uneventful, but tiring. The Panic Bus could barely do fifty-five miles per hour.

As we entered Los Angeles City Limits, I suggested we take a rest stop and visit some old friends of mine in Venice.

Don and Wanda were a couple I had known for years. Don and I had worked together in an electronics factory in Columbus, Nebraska before I moved back to California in 1964.

Don was a big white guy in his early thirties. He was then employed at a giant aerospace corporation in the Inglewood area. He held a management position with the company.

Wanda was a former exotic dancer. She ran a successful African dance studio in Los Angeles. Wanda was born on Halloween in Harlem. She was a "chanting Buddhist", and had a nodding acquaintanceship with the Voodoo religion. She was about thirty, tall and regal-looking. Wanda was a recovering alcoholic with almost five years of A.A. sobriety at that time.

I felt uneasy and irritable as we parked the Panic Bus in front of their modest home. As Lon and I stood on their porch, I tried to control my rising anger. I knocked on the door. "Where is this anger coming from?" I asked myself. Don and Wanda had always been very good friends of mine. There has never been any tension between us. Maybe my tiredness from the long drive was catching up to me.

Wanda opened the door. She whooped in delight and pulled us inside. She hugged me really hard! Don and another couple I had known for several years appeared from the kitchen.

Herman was a large African-American man in his late thirties. He looked like a retired football player. Herman worked with Compton youth gangs. He was wearing a very impressive gemstone amulet. I had never seen Herman wearing anything metaphysical-looking, so I was a bit surprised.

Barbara, Herman's wife, was small and athletic. She was a Sagittarius, and could be very outspoken. Barbara was wearing a long African dress, with her hair in a 'fro. It *was* 1969!

They all looked at each other with a mixture of glee and surprise. Herman boomed. "It worked! I told you it would work!"

I asked, "What worked? What are you talking about? What's going on?"

They became evasive. Herman mumbled something about burying a spoon or a fork in the backyard. They all laughed.

I wasn't laughing. I felt manipulated in some way I didn't understand. Wanda picked up on my discomfort and tried to calm me down. "Relax, Marc. You *knew* you were about to get killed up there".

I tried to be cool and pretend I wasn't freaked-out by what she was saying. Did she somehow tap into my LSD vision of the rednecks raiding our commune? Did she *induce* the vision into my mind because she was worried about us? Did Don, Wanda, Herman, and Barbara focus their energies on us?

I knew they were all seriously concerned about us trying to live a communal life in the Oregon woods.

Don and Wanda had driven up from Los Angeles to visit us in Takilma in the summer of 1968. They only stayed one day. Wanda was terrified of the place, and Don was disgusted by our living conditions. When he needed to go to the bathroom, I handed him a roll of toilet paper, a sawed-off shovel, and pointed him to the forest! They told us we were crazy for living in an area "so beautiful, yet so infested with negativity". They warned us we wouldn't win the local residents over to our way of thinking, and it wasn't our karma to even try.

I began to relax a bit. I knew they were right. I knew their intentions were good, but I didn't understand the metaphysical aspects. The mental picture of a small group of friends in L.A. burying silverware in their backyard and chanting mumbo jumbo in order to influence *my* life up in the forests of Oregon, really irritated me. It frightened me.

I needed to change the subject back to something comforting – something I could somewhat understand – yoga.

"Is the Self-Realization Fellowship Lake Shrine in Pacific Palisades still open to the public?" I asked.

Wanda said, "Yes". There was a moment of uncomfortable silence. Wanda, Herman, and Barbara looked at each other and grinned. This was another one of those telepathic moments. I was shut out of this one, and Don didn't seem to share it, either. He seemed to be pre-occupied with his own thoughts.

"Sure, let's go right now!" Wanda exclaimed excitedly. "We'll take Herman's van".

The thought of visiting the calm, peaceful beauty of the Lake Shrine made me feel safe.

We filed out of Don and Wanda's house, and all found comfortable seating in Herman's spacious new van. Wow! Real seats, air conditioning, and Miles Davis tapes!

As we headed north through Santa Monica, Wanda said, "We need to make a quick stop on the way to Pacific Palisades". She had a sneaky tone-of-voice.

The hairs on the back of my neck stood up. Lon and I looked at each other grimly.

Without a word, Herman pulled the van into the parking lot of a huge building on the ocean side of Pacific Coast Highway. We were on the northern edge of Santa Monica, several miles south of our Pacific Palisades destination.

The big building was the Western Headquarters of the Buddhist cult Don, Wanda, Herman, and Barbara apparently belonged to. I always knew Wanda was a member, but the rest must have recently joined.

Herman turned to Lon and I. "Come on in a minute. There's someone I want you to meet".

We angrily got out of the van and followed Herman into the building. The others stayed in the van. As we entered the building, we were greeted by a Japanese man. He informed us we needed to remove our shoes.

We could see about five hundred pairs of men's shoes arranged neatly in the outer hallway adjacent to the entrance. We removed our shoes and placed them with the others.

Our attention was drawn to a loud, droning HUM, emanating from the next room. It felt and sounded like the hum of a hydro-electrical generator room.

Herman opened the door to the "dynamo room", and motioned us to enter and be seated. Five hundred Asian men were sitting on folding chairs arranged in neat rows. They were all chanting the same mantra I'd heard Wanda chant for years. Every time I would drive up from Costa Mesa to Los Angeles, to visit Don and Wanda, she would chant out loud at least forty-five minutes a day. I had to admit there was a lot of power in that mantra. The sight and sound of five hundred men, chanting it in their native tongue, was very impressive.

Lon and I sat on the floor. There were two reasons we didn't sit on the chairs provided for us. One reason was we were used to sitting on the ground. The second reason was we were being passive-aggressive. We didn't want to be there, but we were too codependent to say, "No" to Don and Wanda.

I assumed a full lotus and began doing a silent meditation of my own. The chanting finally ended, and we all stood and milled around. Herman hurried over to Lon and I. He had an Asian man with him. Herman introduced him as the "district leader", and told us he was anxious to talk to us.

Herman and the district leader hustled us out of the big chanting room and down several flights of stairs.

We found ourselves in the basement of the Headquarters building. The district leader handed me a slip of paper with the four words of their mantra spelled out in English.

"You say these words, you get anything you want!"

When he said that to me I had a flashback to a cold, rainy night in Santa Ana, several years previously. I was drinking in a bar called Jim's Family Inn. Believe me, it was not "family" oriented. I was waiting for the rain to let up, so I could continue home on my chopper. A big black woman walked up to me. I was the only white guy in the bar. She whispered in my ear, "Buddha meeting tonight. Come with me. Where there's Buddha, there's opium". I passed on the Buddha meeting.

Now, I was hearing this, "Chant for anything you want" stuff, and I was really getting pissed off.

I replied to the district leader, "All I want right now is liberation from the wheel of karma". He ignored me. "Five dollars! You chant for five dollars right now! You get five dollars!"

I snapped back, "I don't need five dollars", and growled at Herman to take us back to Don and Wanda's so we could pick up the Panic Bus and finish our journey back to Costa Mesa.

Herman and the district leader were silent as we all trudged back up the stairs. We found our shoes, and put them back on.

Impulsively, Lon yelled, "Imperialists!" at the top of his lungs. He bent over and started mixing up everyone's shoes! I joined in, and we mixed up shoes until they hustled us out the door.

We rode to Don and Wanda's in silence. There was no trip to the Lake Shrine. We arrived at the Panic Bus, and wordlessly climbed out of Herman's van. We slowly got into the VW bus.

A very awkward silence. No hugs. No five-part brotherhood handshakes. We returned to Costa Mesa. Next stop – the Buccaneer Bar, and our real friends, the Buckaroos! We never saw Herman and Barbara, Don and Wanda again.

Chapter 30

ORANGE SUNSHINE

Our Takilma experience behind us, we moved back to Costa Mesa and back to the Buccaneer Bar. Lon, Charlie D, and Hawaiian Joe formed a little country/rock group known as "Charlie D and Milo". Lon also taught guitar to a select few students. I obtained employment at a metaphysical bookstore in Newport Beach. We all chipped-in and rented a small house in Costa Mesa, trying to keep the communal spirit alive.

One of Lon's guitar students was a very straight-appearing aerospace engineer named "Bob". Lon quickly turned Bob on to the Buccaneer, and introduced him to marijuana. "If you want to be a guitar player, Bob, you gotta smoke dope." Before too long, Bob wanted to experience LSD.

I was sitting on my usual barstool at the Buccaneer, next to the jukebox and behind the potato chip rack. Lon, Bob and Joe entered through the back door and found empty barstools next to me. The boys sat down and ordered two pitchers and three glasses.

Lon said, "Hey Marc, this is Bob. He wants to look at The Big Pickup" (our Buccaneer code for dropping acid). Lon continued, "I told him I wasn't doing acid right now, but thought maybe you and Joe could guide him through his first trip. We've got five tabs of Orange Sunshine. The Brotherhood, down in Laguna Beach, told us

103

Tim Leary himself endorses it. He says it is 'imbued with cosmic influences'".

I had to chuckle at Lon's pitch for Orange Sunshine and the Timothy Leary/Brotherhood of Eternal Love endorsement, but was flattered someone wanted me to guide them through their first acid trip. I was also a little scared, having recently experienced some bad trips myself. I was actually thinking about hanging up my psychedelic boots for a while.

In Buckaroo terminology, a "guide" was pretty much a babysitter. The guide watched over the "tripper", ensuring he or she didn't physically hurt themselves or others. If the tripper was in trouble, the guide would attempt to shift the tripper's attention to a higher plane of consciousness.

A guide may or may not take acid with the tripper. Sometimes the guide would take a lower dose of the same type of acid, attempting to maintain a compatible wavelength to the tripper. We'd all heard horror stories of guides mind-fucking their trippers, either out of sadism or a desire to bring the tripper under their control. The Buckaroo unwritten/unspoken code-of-conduct was: "Do no harm to the tripper." I agreed to team up with Joe and be Bob's guide.

Five orange tablets seemed to magically appear on a bar napkin next to Bob's pitcher. I cast a furtive glance around the bar to make sure CIA Jeff wasn't present, then scooped up two of the orange tablets and washed them down with my Schlitz. Bob took one tab. Joe took one tab. I don't know what became of the fifth tablet. Without comment, we finished our pitchers and headed for the parking lot. It was around ten in the evening.

Lon was playing a gig that night, so he left by himself in the blue Panic Bus.

ORANGE SUNSHINE

I slid behind the wheel of "Buck", my 1964 Chevrolet El Camino, and fired it up. The "327" engine, unmodified except for a AFB four-barrel carburetor and headers, sounded especially sweet. I thought, "Oh my God, this Orange Sunshine shit is coming on already!"

Bob and Joe followed me out of the parking lot in Bob's Mustang Cobra. It was a good thing our communally-rented house was only a few blocks from the Buccaneer. The living room walls and ceiling were already breathing as we entered the animated cartoon-looking front door.

We silently sat cross-legged on the floor and waited to see what would happen next. The acid was coming on hard and fast.

"How am I going to be anyone's guide?", I thought. "It looks like I'm going to be hanging on to my ass for dear life!"

I tried to appear calm and composed as I glanced over at Joe. He met my gaze with an, "Oh, shit!" look in his eyes. We looked at Bob, then back at each other. Bob was changing! Joe and I both saw it happening. Bob's forehead became really tall. He started rocking back and forth, softly chanting, "The others are coming...the others are coming..." Visions of UFOs in deep space appeared before my mind's eye.

Bob jumped to his feet and began to give a sermon on the nature of reality. He sounded as if he was channeling Paramahansa Yogananda or some other great Yogi of the past.

Bob could read our minds! Whoever or whatever he had become was now pulling dirty shameful secret thoughts out of our minds and feeding them back to us in a weird sing-song chanting voice. Joe and I excused ourselves and went into another room to re-group. Bob followed us, continuing his way-too-personal spiritual discourse. We tried to maintain our calm exteriors throughout this unending psychedelic storm.

"Bob" took a short break from his telepathic shame-a-thon, and non-verbally instructed us in the formation of a three-man masonic-like hand-grip. I felt we were now connected into some sort of triangular biochemical/electrical circuit. Using our energy like extra batteries, "Bob" seemed to be communicating to an extra-terrestrial intelligence "out there" somewhere.

What remained of Joe and my identities telepathically made an agreement. "Well, it doesn't seem like whatever took over Bob is going to kill us, so let's just ride it out." Shortly before dawn, "Bob" began to slow down a bit, but he was still transmitting and receiving unintelligible cosmic information.

I flashed on an idea. "Let's take Bob for a ride! We need to get out of this house and get in the wind". Joe nodded enthusiastically. Bob handed me the keys to his Mustang without a word. The early morning air felt cool and clean. The sun was just peeking over the horizon. "Sun come up today. Good omen", I thought to myself.

Bob climbed into the tiny back seat on his Mustang. Joe rode shotgun. As I drove aimlessly around the Costa Mesa-Newport Beach area, I could feel "Bob" sending electrical impulses through my medulla oblongata.

Bob's Mustang seemed to want to go out to the Irvine Industrial Complex, near Orange County Airport. I gave the Mustang its head. We pulled into a deserted parking lot adjacent to a vast aerospace complex surrounded by a high chain-link fence topped with barbed-wire. We faced a large open field. Visible through the fence were spooky-looking antennas of varied shapes and sizes. Vertical towers and huge satellite dishes were scattered throughout the field. The area looked like a set from a very expensive and realistic science-fiction movie. I observed a small sign on the fence, "Collins Radio Company".

I had unconsciously brought us to a very sophisticated and powerful aerospace communications network, just the ticket for ol' Bob! Maybe it really was, because he calmed down quickly. Perhaps the acid was finally wearing off, or perhaps the energy from all those radio towers overloaded the circuitry of whatever he was channeling, but Bob returned to normal.

We all know, of course, one never completely returns to one's old self after a heavy acid experience.

I cranked up the Mustang and burned rubber out of the Collins Radio Company parking lot. It was time to open up the Buccaneer!

Bob was now a Buckaroo of *high degree*.

Chapter 31

SUNNY VALLEY

When our little group left Takilma and moved back to Costa Mesa in early 1969, we abandoned some of our meager material possessions. By June, I was ready to go back for them.

Two other Buckaroos, Bob and Wayne, wanted to go along. They wanted to visit a commune near Medford, Oregon; an area called Sunny Valley.

Some of our original Takilma commune, including Ron, Nancy and their kids, split off from our group in late 1968, and joined a forest commune near Sunny Valley. Bob and Wayne somehow contacted them and asked if we could come up and visit their group. Once again, I got one of those uneasy feelings.

There were reports in the hippie underground; a commune near Sunny Valley was into witchcraft and "earth magick".

I really liked Ron and Nancy, and was very surprised when they joined the Sunny Valley group. I wasn't really sure if this was the same "witchy" bunch I'd heard about. Regardless, it would be good to see them again, so I agreed to go. Sunny Valley was only about a two-hour drive from Takilma. I could pick up my stuff on Takilma Road, then go see Ron and Nancy. It would be fun.

ORANGE SUNSHINE

We left Costa Mesa on June nineteenth, in Bob's Mustang Cobra. I picked up the few things I valued in Takilma, loaded them in Bob's tiny trunk and we arrived in Sunny Valley on the Summer Solstice.

We drove to a remote location about thirty miles from Medford. Representatives from the commune were waiting for us. Ron was among the group, and greeted me with a big hippie hug and a mini-keg of Michelob. He appeared much more primitive-looking now. One would never guess that only eighteen months earlier, he had been a computer science professor at University of California, Irvine, with a wife and kids, and a lovely home near the campus. His red beard was well below his chest. He was very thin and wild-eyed, but I was really glad to see him.

We all stood around our vehicles, drinking beer and introducing ourselves to each other. After about twenty minutes of socializing on this rural backroad, Bob, Wayne and I piled back into the Mustang.

The guys from the Sunny Valley group climbed into Ron's old VW bus. Ron's old VW bus! A flood of memories... it seemed so long ago, but it was only two years previously we were riding in that same bus to the June 23, 1967 anti-war demonstration in Century Plaza, Los Angeles. Now we hardly knew each other.

We followed Ron's bus onto a narrow one-lane logging road, winding and climbing through the thick forest. After about five miles, the unpaved logging road narrowed to no road, and we stopped.

A handful of cars, vans, and a pickup truck were parked in a small clearing. Bob negotiated the Mustang into the clearing. We parked, and got out of the car, ducking under tree branches.

We joined the others, who were waiting for us. Although I had lived in the forest in Takilma for a year, with no electricity, no running water, no outhouse, and no house, I felt like a city slicker compared to these psychedelic tribesmen.

We followed Ron and his group along a trail leading deeper into the forest. It was a pretty good climb as well. After what seemed like a mile or so of hiking the narrow trail, we came to another clearing. Several other members of the commune were waiting for us. More introductions all around. Ron introduced me as "the guy who turned us on exactly two years ago". He had a slightly accusatory tone-of-voice. He looked like Ron, but he didn't *feel* like Ron.

One of the other guys mumbled something back to Ron. "Mumble mumble...the guy we've been expecting...mumble mumble...summer solstice...mumble mumble...he's the Cancer-Leo...mumble mumble"

Ron asked me if I still did psychedelics. I had been hoping he wouldn't ask me that. My recent Orange Sunshine experience with Joe and Bob was enough to cause me to want to take another break from psychedelics. My nervous system was still shaking from that trip. Like a fool, I said, "Sure!" I thought they'd think I was weak if I refused. Ron said, "Good. A member of our Family just returned from South America with a little something he obtained from a witch doctor down there. He says there's nothing like it on *this* planet. I said, 'Great". I thought, "Oh, fuck!"

Ron and the other guys from Sunny Valley looked at each other and smiled. "Wayne, Bob, you guys wanna trip, too?" Wayne and Bob nodded cautiously.

"Follow us. We'll take the medicine at our sacred spot; then we'll go down and introduce you to the rest of the Family. I want you to meet them before it gets dark".

We followed Ron and his little crew up a winding path into the hills. As we continued climbing, the forest thinned out a bit. Altogether, there was Wayne, Bob, myself, plus Ron and four of the Sunny Valley men.

At the top of the hill, I noticed a big stone altar, a drum, and five logs arranged to form a pentagon.

We were instructed to sit on the logs, facing the interior of the pentagon. We all sat down. One of their guys stood in the center of the pentagon. He dramatically produced a leather medicine bag, and told us to hold out our left hands, palms up. We did so. He stood in front of me and asked, "How many? One, or two?" I replied, "Two".

He poured the powdered contents of two capsules onto my open left palm, and said, "Just hold it there". He went around the pentagon. I remember Wayne took "One", but don't remember how much anyone else took. I was already beginning to feel weird.

A thought struck me. "Oh, shit! These people are following a dark, left-handed Path!" I immediately tried to transfer the powdered drug from my left hand to my right hand, hoping I could reverse the polarity of the trip – at least as far as I was concerned.

Their "medicine man" gave us further instructions: "Now lick the powder off your palms. You will ingest what hasn't been absorbed."

We all licked the remainder of the drug from our open palms. Now, I was feeling really stoned and very anxious. I wished I were back at the Buccaneer, drinking beer, eating potato chips, and listening to Janis Joplin on the jukebox.

We didn't get to sit in the pentagon very long. Ron and his coven of warlocks all stood up at exactly the same time, as if they were wired together.

We Buckaroos struggled to our feet and followed the Sunny Valley group back down the trail. The sun was setting, and I was kicking myself for even coming up here.

We finally arrived at the Sunny Valley commune. It was much larger than I thought it would be. A longhouse constructed of logs was the most noticeable structure. "It must be their Lodge", I thought. Tepees were scattered throughout the forest.

Approximately forty adults stood in a circle, around a large open fire. I didn't see any children, but I knew there were lots of kids in the commune. Ron and Nancy had four kids of their own – well, not really "their own". Ron explained they had all dissolved their marriages and were now all married to each other. Thus, the kids were all raised communally. No more bourgeois "mommy and daddy". When I heard this, I felt angry and disgusted, but the drug was overpowering my conscious mind, and I was fighting to keep my circuits from overloading.

We were asked to join the circle. Everyone held hands. I felt comforted because I thought we were going to pray or give thanks – something wholesome and familiar. I could feel the energy going around the circle. It was powerful, and I liked it at first.

Someone started chanting, "OM". I thought, "OM is good. I can do OM". As we continued to chant, the energy became more powerful. Then, someone made a loud animal sound. Someone else responded with another, more guttural noise. I could "hear" members of the group communicating telepathically with each other. Suddenly, I became ill. I had to break their circle and stumble off into the woods to throw up. Ron came over, and asked if I was alright. I nodded, and stood up shakily.

Ron told all of us who took the psychedelic to follow him to the "sacred tepee", where our magical trip would take place.

We followed Ron and the Sunny Valley trippers up another trail to a lone tepee, isolated from the others. I figured it must be used for ceremonies such as this.

It was now night, and very dark when we entered the tepee. A small fire in the center gave off enough light for us to find our way around inside. We all took our seats on the ground, around the fire. The drug had really taken effect! Whatever it was, felt like a combination of LSD and peyote. This might have been a good trip in familiar surroundings, with loving friends, but these folks were acting as if they had a hidden agenda with us. They were very earthy and witchy.

Wayne checked-out early, and lay down by himself, as if to sleep. The Sunny Valley group then seemed to turn their attention to me. I had the feeling this meeting had been planned for a long time, that it was to coincide with the summer solstice, and that they wanted me to join their group, or somehow give my energy to it. If that was true, I didn't like the way they were recruiting me.

I could feel their psychic energy pulling on me. I didn't understand what they were doing. I tried to meditate. I closed my eyes and focused my attention at the third eye, that point inside the forehead, between and a little above, the two eyes. At the same time, I mentally repeated a Sanskrit mantra. Within a few seconds, the energy in the tepee changed. I felt the Sunny Valley group's discomfort. It reminded me of a horror movie, when someone throws Holy Water on the vampire.

They responded to my attempt to meditate with a psychic blast that dropped my attention to the lower chakras. I assumed a full lotus posture, and brought my focus back to the third eye. More groans and pained responses from the commune members.

A woman entered the tepee carrying a burning stick. She drew occult symbols in the air with the flaming stick. Another woman came in and read some shit from a witchcraft book. My attention dropped again, and there was an audible sigh of relief from their group. I closed my eyes and ears to the distractions and raised my attention again. The women left the tepee, and the energy duel continued on for hours. I became tired of being ganged-up on, and did something dramatic. I stuck my bare feet into the fire, and held them there. In my altered state, I *believed* I had synchronized the vibratory rate of my feet to the vibratory rate of the fire. My feet didn't burn. The Sunny Valley boys made more groaning sounds. I was really getting tired. I took my feet out of the fire after a voice in my head said, "Don't press your luck, Marc".

Just then, Bob jumped into the action. It was wild! His forehead got really tall again, and his lower jaw got…different. He looked like an alien. "Bob" began pulling very personal thoughts out of everyone's mind, and feeding these thoughts back to them in the now familiar, unearthly sing-song voice. Their little coven appeared quite disturbed and disrupted. "Bob" didn't let up, and one by one, they all dropped out of the circle and crashed.

When the Sunny Valley group had all "fallen asleep", Bob and I woke up Wayne, and we quietly exited the tepee. I felt a real sense of urgency to get out of there as quickly and quietly as possible.

ORANGE SUNSHINE

The sun was rising. We located the Mustang. Wayne collapsed in the back seat. Bob let me drive. The Ambassador from Saturn hadn't completely vacated Bob's body yet!

We re-traced our route back to Interstate 5, and drove straight back to Costa Mesa, California. To this day, I don't know what the whole thing was all about. Bob, Wayne and I never discussed the experience.

Chapter 32

MANLY PALMER HALL

The study of yoga and Eastern mysticism reminded me of my brief career in Freemasonry. Much of what I had experienced in my Nebraska Masonic Lodge obviously had roots in Eastern philosophy. Should I return to Freemasonry and give it another try?

I was deeply troubled by one aspect of Freemasonry. At that time, Masonic Lodges in America were racially segregated. The white lodges were mostly made up of white Christians, Jews, and Native Americans. The black, or "Prince Hall" lodges were composed solely of African-American men. Why weren't the lodges totally integrated? I decided to consult one of the world's most prominent authorities on Freemasonry, Secret Societies, and Ancient Mystery Schools.

Manly Palmer Hall, Thirty-Third Degree Mason, world famous author, and founder of the Philosophical Research Society, lived and taught right here in Los Angeles. I called his secretary, and asked for a personal interview, "to discuss Masonic matters". I was granted the interview but had to wait nine days. I fasted those nine days, drinking only distilled water and herbal tea. I thought I was preparing myself to meet an occult Master.

The interview was held in his office at the Philosophical Research Society, a truly impressive place. I identified myself as "having been raised to the Sublime Degree of Master Mason", then directly asked him why the white lodges and the black lodges weren't integrated. His answer didn't satisfy me. He either did not have an answer that made sense to me or his answer went over my head and I didn't understand him. When I tried to get clarification, I became more confused. I thanked him for his time and left, feeling disappointed and irritated. I decided not to re-instate my membership at that time.

Chapter 33

ASTROLOGY AND THE MANSON TRIAL

"What Sign are you, man?" That seemed to be the question one was asked immediately after names were exchanged in the late sixties and early seventies. "I'm Little Tree and I'm Aquarius", or, "My name is Lisa. I'm a Libra. I'm six years old and I smoke grass with my mom and dad"

Well, I didn't *know* what sign I was, "man"! My fellow hippies were very disturbed I didn't know my own astrological sign. Most of them had their charts "done" by astrologers and at least knew their Sun Signs, Moon Signs, and Rising Signs.

The reason I didn't know my birth sign was I was born exactly between two signs. My hippie friends told me, "You were born on the cusp, man. Far out!" My cusp is between Cancer and Leo (July 23). Some of my friends said I was a Cancer; some said, "You've got to be a Leo, man!" I have to admit I was curious.

My educational background, such as it was, was fairly left-brain. Lots of math and science in high school, and some college math and geology. I thought astrology was for eccentric little old ladies and hippie space cadets.

I was interested in yoga and eastern philosophy, however. Karma, reincarnation, and astrology have been taken very seriously in Asia for thousands of years. I didn't want to completely discount a subject I hadn't studied, and knew nothing about; that would be arrogant and stupid.

In December 1969, I signed up for an astrology class. The classes were being held at a bookstore on the Balboa Peninsula in Newport Beach. We met one night a week, three hours per class. The beginning class was fifteen weeks.

I learned how to calculate the positions of the sun, moon, and planets in relation to any geographical location at any moment in time. A natal horoscope is a map of the solar system over the longitude and latitude of the newborn baby, when she or he takes the first breath outside the womb – at that exact time. Learning how to "cast a chart" was much more complicated than I thought. I did find out I *was* born on the Cancer-Leo cusp, four astrological minutes on the Cancer side.

The second fifteen weeks, we learned the basics of interpreting the natal chart. We learned the unique qualities of each planet, the twelve "houses" of a chart, and the aspects, or angular relationships between the planets. In those fifteen weeks, we barely scratched the surface. I was now beginning to gain a little more respect for this ancient art.

The third fifteen weeks, we learned a little about transits and progressions. This class taught us how to relate current or future planetary positions to the natal horoscope. The purpose of this class was to enable us to use this information in making major personal decisions – very much like a sailor using a tide table and weather reports to plan a voyage.

The classes were interesting and fun. We calculated the charts of famous people, and our teacher helped us interpret the charts. The teacher was an aerospace systems analyst as well as a highly respected astrologer. Among his clients were some Wall Street millionaires.

I continued with more classes throughout 1970, and during the time of the trial of Charles Manson. I thought it would be very cool if I could somehow provide the class with the data necessary to cast the chart of Mr. Manson. I needed to obtain his time, date, and place of birth.

My friend, and Buckaroo of *high degree*, Jerry, was planning to attend the trial. I don't know why. He didn't seem all that interested in the case. I asked him a small favor, "Hey, Jerry, if the opportunity comes up, could you somehow get Manson's birth info?" Jerry lit up like a Christmas Tree. He was on a mission! I'd already done Jerry's chart, so he knew what I was talking about.

The following evening, Jerry returned to the Buccaneer white-faced and shaken. He reported he did get into the courtroom as a spectator. At some point, during a short recess, he was able to speak to Mr. Manson's attorney. Jerry asked for the birth information. The attorney approached Manson, who asked, "Who wants to know?" The attorney pointed to Jerry. Charles Manson and Jerry locked eyes; that got the judge's attention, and the judge and Jerry locked eyes.

Jerry told me later, there was something "likable" about Mr. Manson. The feeling must have been mutual, because Jerry obtained the birth data through Mr. Manson's attorney. Jerry didn't get such a likable feeling from the judge.

After the day's court proceedings, Jerry was walking back to his car, when he was suddenly surrounded by deputies. They pounced upon poor Jerry and hustled him roughly back into the courthouse. He was dragged into a small room full of deputies, and the world famous Judge Older.

They demanded to know what was going on. Jerry simply told them the truth. They didn't believe Jerry, and searched him. When they emptied Jerry's pockets they found an Arabic coin. That got them all excited! Jerry had dark hair, a moustache, and a ruddy complexion. I think they made a somewhat paranoid mental leap, and saw Jerry as some kind of Sirhan Sirhan character.

The deputies and the judge finally determined Jerry was clean, but he was most harshly ordered never to show his face in that courtroom again.

I presented this hard-won birth data to my astrology teacher and classmates, but I did not tell them the whole story.

Charles Manson's natal chart indicated no contact with his natural father, early separation from his mother, and an abundance of personal magnetism and sexual energy.

According to his horoscope, he could have been either a great healer and spiritual teacher, or...the infamous Charlie Manson.

Chapter 34

CIRCLING THE WANT ADS

I seem to have a very deep work ethic buried in my DNA. If I'm not working, I feel pretty worthless as a human being and as a man.

There were several periods, however, when I was between jobs and *wanted* to remain between jobs. If I had drinking money I was OK. During these rare periods of unemployment, I spent as much time at the Buccaneer or Dick's Horseshoe Saloon as was possible with my limited funds.

I considered my drinking buddies to be my "real family". They didn't judge me – tortured, sensitive, not-of-this-earth soul that I was.

Looking back over these periods, I see I was not only alcoholic, but probably clinically depressed as well.

I drank all day and played the jukebox if I had the money. I listened to my favorite songs over and over: *I Can Still Hear The Music In The Restroom*, by Jerry Lee Lewis; *Swingin' Doors*, by Merle Haggard, or anything mournful by Hank Williams.

I was always in a relationship. My significant other also worked and assumed responsibility for writing the checks, balancing the checkbook, and paying the bills. My duty was to contribute a large portion of my paycheck – every week- to keep *her* off my back. I would hold back the rest of my pay for alcohol and other drugs. But – no work – no paycheck.

I could always sense when my not-working was just about to get me evicted from the relationship. At that critical point, this is what I would do:

I'd wait until she left for work in the morning, then run to the liquor store and buy the *Orange County Register* – our daily newspaper – and a six pack of beer. Returning home with the newspaper, I'd have a beer, and tear out the "Employment Opportunities" section. As I finished my six-pack, I would take a pen and circle every job I was qualified for. After I finished that task, I'd fold the paper in such a way that these circled ads were visible. I left the neatly folded paper next to the phone. Off to the Buccaneer or Dick's Horseshoe!

I always felt creepy, but a guy's got to do what a guy's got to do. This obviously sincere attempt to find work would usually buy me another week or two of morbid, depressed unemployment.

When I was really up against the wall and my circling the "Help Wanted" ads scam had expired, I'd move to phase two. I would actually go to a big aerospace company, such as Douglas Aircraft in Long Beach, and bring home an application. I would fill out the application, with a very serious face, in front of my significant other. Naturally, I would need more time off and would not seek inferior employment. I must return the completed application to the company and await their response. The wages and benefits would be worth it.

Another several weeks on my barstool without a response from one of these companies and I would have to go back to work – for real.

Chapter 35

THE KIVA

Jon R, another Buckaroo of *high degree*, found himself alone in his house in Costa Mesa one morning in 1972. His wife and kids left him and moved to San Diego County. We were sad for Jon, but happy for us. We Buckaroos now had a house we could hide out in when we were estranged from our significant others, or when the *man* was looking for us. Buckaroos tended to have more misunderstandings with law enforcement than most Costa Mesa residents.

Greedy capitalist employers often refused to see our special tortured genius qualities. Buckaroos were sometimes between jobs.

We began to think of ourselves as Native Americans, and Jon's house became our sacred kiva, where we held our manly ceremonies. We really weren't too far off on the Native American concept. Our regular kiva initiates were: Joe, a Native American; Dave D, a Mexican-American; Jerry had an ex-wife who was Native American from Oklahoma; I'm one-eighth Cherokee, and Jon R was either Native American/Irish or Hawaiian/Irish! Real Buckaroos didn't discuss their "feelings", or their families of origin.

Our sacred ceremony began by meeting at John's house every workday at eleven in the morning. We arranged the couches and armchairs into a semi-circle around the sacred television.

Traditional ceremonial firearms were stacked in a corner – A .30 caliber M-1 carbine; two twelve-gauge riot guns, and a .45 caliber fully automatic tommy gun.

Once seated comfortably, we fired up multiple joints of marijuana, imported from Columbia, and purchased by me at Eddie's Sandbox, an African-American bar in Long Beach. During this phase of my life, I was smoking marijuana again. I wasn't concerned about stimulating my lower chakras. On special occasions, I'd bring over some of my homemade marijuana brownies. Jon called them, "Mother Marc's Magical Muffins". I was miffed at the "mother" moniker.

To further exercise and stimulate our minds, we practiced multi-tasking by simultaneously passing around a freshly opened bottle of cheap whiskey, while, at the same time, joints were going around the room clockwise *and* counter-clockwise.

Topping it all off, from twelve noon to one in the afternoon, we watched *All My Children* religiously. We rarely missed an episode. Erika Kane and Nick Davis were like friends to us.

At one o'clock, after *All My Children,* we ceremonially closed the kiva, and convoyed the three blocks to the Buccaneer Bar. We found our special barstools, and sat with great dignity, explaining the nature of reality to Buckaroos of *low degree* and Buckaroo wannabees.

Chapter 36

THE ALAMO CLUB

I don't remember why I was *walking* down Placentia Street in Costa Mesa on a particular morning in 1973. My trusty 1964 Chevrolet El Camino, "Buck", must have been in the shop for repairs. Placentia Street, in those days, had a drinking establishment located about every half block. I was drunk, walking, checking out all the bars. I thought I knew them all from years of driving through the neighborhood, but it appeared there was one I had previously missed.

It looked like a beer bar. There was a little parking lot in front and probably a bigger lot in back. I thought the sign on the front of the bar read "Alamo Club". I was very excited! It must be a country bar with a great jukebox full of Hank Williams, George Jones, and Bob Wills music. With a name like the Alamo Club, it must be a hard-drinking, two-fisted, shit-kicking, open-at-six-in the morning, redneck bar.

I walked through the door and froze. Everyone was standing around drinking coffee! They were smiling and laughing. No jukebox. It was very creepy. Through my alcoholic impaired perception, everyone looked like they were wearing golf clothes. Bumper stickers were plastered all over the walls: "Take it Easy"; "One Day at a Time", "Let Go and Let God". Aieeeee! The Alamo

Club was a meeting place for recovering alcoholics! Arghhhh! I could feel the sobriety like a vampire feels sunlight.

I barely escaped as one of them approached me, smiling. Outside, and safe from recovery, I looked at the sign again. "Alano Club – like, short for Alcoholics Anonymous.

I would visit the Alano Club again in a few years, so I guess this would be, in screenwriter talk, a foreshadowing.

Chapter 37

THE VEGAS ROOM

The Buccaneer Bar and Dick's Horseshoe Saloon weren't the only bars I frequented in Costa Mesa. There was also Bay Street, the Fling, Hearn's, Little John's, the Shamrock, The Road's End, and many, many others. I just felt more at home at the "Buc" and Dick's.

The Vegas Room was a small neighborhood bar on the west side of Costa Mesa. It had the best country music jukebox in town – lots of classic cry-in-your-beer tunes.

The local Marine Corps recruiter and I were sitting next to each other at the bar. We were both very drunk. He was in uniform. I was raving on about the current state of the Vietnam War. This was in the early seventies, and the war was going badly. Public support of the war was diminishing, and the country was polarized. We argued. His face got red, and I became personal in my verbal attack. I told the Marine he had wasted his life killing third world people to make the *man* richer.

His karate chop to the front of my throat sent me flying backwards off my barstool. I landed on my back. My glasses lay on the floor next to me. I was grateful they hadn't broken. I put them back on. I was stunned but not really hurt. Several customers helped me to my feet. I got back on my barstool.

The Marine recruiter had moved to the other end of the bar. Most of the customers were mad at the Marine. That really surprised me.

"He's a disgrace to the uniform", someone proclaimed loudly. I played the tape back in my head. *I* was the disgrace for telling this old alcoholic, overdue-for-retirement Marine his life was a waste, and worse than meaningless. What did I know about this man, the wars he had fought, the comrades he had lost, the brave things he had done?

I got off my barstool and went over to him and apologized. He looked shocked and ashamed. We shook hands, and I returned to my barstool. I was very quiet the remainder of the night.

I stopped by the Vegas Room now and then over the next few years, when I was in the mood to hear that great country jukebox, but never saw the old Marine again. The whole experience was depressing. My little party at the Vegas Room, was over.

Chapter 38

MY LITTLE RED STORY

The shame, frustration and anger over our failed attempt to create a utopian community in Oregon, and the continuing nightmare of the war in Vietnam drove me deeper into political radicalism.

The assassinations of the Kennedys and Martin Luther King contributed to my belief we were living in a post *coup d'etat* State. I was not then, not have I ever been, interested in becoming a liberal. I wanted to actively participate in " bringing it all down".

I put on my blue work shirt, my black steel-toed combat boots, and went back to work in the factories and machine shops of Orange and Los Angeles Counties.

At the same time, and at the opposite end of the philosophical universe, two men from our old Takilma group told me they'd finally found a real Guru. He was known as a Perfect Living Master, and lived in the Punjab of northern India – near the Pakistan border. They said He did not proselytize, advertise, or accept money for His Teachings. He was scheduled to give a discourse in Pasadena in 1970. My two friends went to Pasadena, connected with the Sat Guru, and received Initiation into this very strict and little-known Path of meditation. I was afraid to go with them, and chose to get drunk that particular day. I was interested, but not ready.

My first move into a political organization came near the beginning of the seventies. I joined the Industrial Workers of the World. The I.W.W. had a long colorful history in America. They were old-time anarchists. I loved their slogans: "Workers of the World Unite, You Have Nothing To Lose But Your Chains!" and "An Injury to One is an Injury to All!" My favorite slogan was, "I'd Rather Be Called Red than Yellow!"

As a now self-proclaimed anarchist and card-carrying member of the I.W.W., I never went to any meetings, organized any workers, or improved conditions in anyone's life. On a very active political day I might write one of their slogans on the restroom wall of a bar – right above the urinal – at eye level.

I never really connected to the I.W.W., so I moved on to the Vietnam Veterans Against the War.

My own period of military service was an eight-year obligation, which included Nebraska National Guard, active duty U.S. Army, and Army Reserve.

I signed-up in December 1959, while still in high school, and was actually called out of the classroom to fight a flood on the Platte River. I was seventeen.

In June 1960, immediately after high school graduation, I was activated into the Army. My Military Occupational Specialty was 111.00 Light Weapons Infantry. It was my M.O.S. of choice.

Most of the weapons I trained and qualified with are now obsolete: M1 Garand; M1 and M2 Carbine; .45 Model 1911 semi-automatic pistol; Browning Automatic Rifle (the BAR was my favorite weapon); .30 Cal. Light Machine Gun; 3.5 Rocket Launcher; and the very scary flame thrower.

I didn't like the Army. I was emotionally immature, poorly coordinated physically, and had a terrible attitude. I stayed out of trouble, however, and received my Honorable Discharge in December 1967, upon completion of the last of my Army Reserve time. The final two years of Army Reserve was Inactive Duty. My name was on a list and I was subject to re-call at the whim of the *man.*

I did not serve in Vietnam, but the Vietnam Veterans Against the War allowed me to join because I was a "Vietnam era" veteran. Close enough! I fit in well with the other angry ex-G.I.s. Most of us had long hair and beards, and in our military fatigues or cammos, we looked like Cuban revolutionaries.

A Vietnam Veterans Against the War convention was held in San Luis Obisbo, California. I was one of the Orange County delegates. It was a fun and interesting trip. Several of the delegates wore red stars on their fatigue caps. Upon inquiry, I was told these men also belonged to another radical group called the Venceremos Brigade. I liked the sound of that name!

The Venceremos Brigade had strong ties to the Communist Party of Cuba. The V.B. trained angry and idealistic young people to "help in the sugar harvest" in Cuba, and learn revolution. It sounded very romantic. I thought of the Abraham Lincoln Brigade, sending American volunteers into Spain to fight fascism prior to World War Two.

The small, multi-racial Venceremos Brigade group I was associated with, met regularly in the *barrios* of Santa Ana. Our larger regional meetings were held in Los Angeles, in an old building near MacArthur Park. I remember a red steel door with a peephole, and a sign over the door, "Ballet Studio". They told us the place had been firebombed several times by anti-Castro Cubans.

They also said the building, and all of us, were being watched by the F.B.I., and the L.A.P.D.'s mysterious Red Squad. The name "Omega-7" was mentioned in reference to the anti-Castro Cubans.

Our group of *brigadistas* was training to go on the next trip to Cuba. We were to travel by bus into Mexico and fly to Cuba from there. We were told we would return through Canada.

The Venceremos Brigade held a big fund-raiser for the Cuba trip at a famous folk music club on Melrose Avenue in Hollywood. Revolutionary singers, poets, and musicians performed. At the end we all took up the chant, "Pick up the gun, put the pig on the run!" I wondered who the agent provocateur was that came up with *that* slogan for us to chant in front of the *man* in our midst! It made me very uncomfortable.

Our Venceremos Brigade leaders tried to teach us Cuban history and a little practical Spanish. Nothing fancy.

My dad died just prior to our departure for Cuba, and I made the difficult decision to stay home.

I met with the *brigadistas* upon their return eight weeks later. They were fresh from their training, and told me they had a great time. I was jealous when I heard they had an audience with the Maximum Leader, Fidel Castro!

I felt regret I didn't go, but at the same time, I was becoming disenchanted with the Venceremos Brigade.

It appeared there were two major revolutionary paths available in the early to mid-seventies: the way of the Soviet Union and it's gang in the United States, the Communist Party USA; or the way of Chairman Mao and the "glorious and heroic" Peoples Republic of China.

It seemed to me the original revolutionary ideals of Lenin and the Russian Revolution had been corrupted under Stalin – if not before. According to my simplistic thinking, the Communist Party USA, the Communist Party of Cuba, and thus, the Venceremos Brigade, were all under the influence of the revisionist Communist Party USSR. I did not want to align myself with the Soviet Union.

The purest revolutionary thinking, in my opinion at the time, came from Chairman Mao and the Peoples Republic of China.

I attended anti-war, and other radical demonstrations in Los Angeles until I connected with a group called the "October League". They were connected to the Peoples Republic of China and believed the social- imperialist USSR was the main enemy of world peace, followed by the U.S. capitalist-imperialists, of course.

The October League had their own weekly newspaper, *The Call,* which was printed in English and Spanish. As soon as I joined the October League, I began to distribute *The Call* in Long Beach and Orange County.

Headquarters for the October League was in Chicago, but they were very well organized in Los Angeles. The October League was actually building a new Party, the Communist Party Marxist-Leninist.

I jumped on board. The Communist Party Marxist-Leninist had very strict rules of behavior for its cadre. No drugs, no getting drunk, and no sexual relations with the workers we were trying to recruit. We were all heterosexual men and women. The Cubans and the Chinese Communists were, at that time, outspoken in their disapproval of homosexuality.

May 25, 1974, I began a period of abstinence from alcohol and other drugs. I remained dry for two years and two months. I moved to the South Gate/East Los Angeles area and pretended to do "factory organizing" wherever I worked. I was a terrible labor organizer. The poor, mostly undocumented, workers I was trying to organize and radicalize, just wanted to be left alone to follow the American Dream.

The October League/Communist Party Marxist-Leninist had meetings every week. We had to report our progress recruiting "advanced workers" in our factories. We also engaged in criticism/self-criticism sessions on the subject of how well we were living *our* lives according to Marxist-Leninist principles. Does our "practice" match our "theory"?

We were only introduced to the members of our own cell. We didn't know members of other cells, or even how many cells the Party had in the Los Angeles District.

We had to participate in a "Marxist-Leninist Mao Tse Tung Thought" study group once a week. We read and discussed "the classics": Marx and Engels; Mao's *Four Essays on Philosophy* and *Combat Liberalism*; Stalin's *Dialectical and Historical Materialism*; and, of course, we endlessly discussed articles from *Iskra,* written in the early 1900s by Vladimir Ilich Ulyanov (Lenin), as if they were current and relevant!

The study groups and cell meetings were held at different locations in East Los Angeles each week. We were never to arrive as a group, but straggled into the meetings one person at a time.

I was never able to swallow the Party line, and could never actually visualize another revolution in the United States of America. I think I was drawn to being part of something I considered to be internationally "heavy" and dangerous.

The primary contradiction within myself was between the political and the spiritual. Part of me wanted to make a difference, to help change the world, to " sweep the beach", to "plow the sea". The other part was seeking inner peace and a unity with the Higher Power that transcends this ephemeral region of duality.

Chapter 39

LONDON 1976

In late June 1976, I flew to London on Dan Air out of LAX. The purpose of my trip was to see the Sat Guru from India I had refused to see in Pasadena in 1970. He was going to be in London for several weeks, then return to the Punjab. I regretted not seeing Him in 1970, and had heard He rarely visited the West. This was my chance to see a real Saint outside of India.

By coincidence, I arrived in England on the Summer Solstice, and was able to get to Stonehenge for the celestial event. In those days, one could actually walk around inside the stone circle, or sit and meditate right on the site! Some of the tourists said it felt creepy or scary inside the circle. I didn't get that feeling, but maybe I *wanted* it to feel powerful and mysterious, not creepy.

I was also in London at the same time as the Bi-Centennial of the United States of America, July Fourth 1976. The gift shops and tourist traps were full of USA Bi-Centennial flags, coffee mugs, T-shirts, etc. I had to laugh. Here they are, celebrating *our* independence from them, and our defeat of them in the American Revolution. I couldn't help but love the British for their cool attitude.

At this stage of my life I was in a total split. On one hand, I followed a strict lacto-vegetarian diet. I used no alcohol or other drugs. I meditated two and one-half hours every morning before sunrise, and was trying to lead a clean ethical life.

On the other hand, I was still active in the October League/Communist Party Marxist-Leninist. My Maoist comrades would have been beyond upset if they knew I was involved with any form of spirituality. They claimed to be atheists and materialists.

Somehow I was able to reconcile Mao Tse Tung Thought with Eastern mysticism, at least for a while.

One afternoon, in London, I attended the spiritual discourse of the Sat Guru. The event was held at Earls Court, and the place was packed. I wept as the Sat Guru explained this world is not our Home. The soul has wandered in the creation since the beginning of time, moving from one body to the next, life after life, until it tires of the creation and yearns to go back to the Creator, and its True Home with God.

Immediately after the discourse, I dried my tears, bolted for the door, ran to the subway, and headed to Golders Green for a Communist Party Meeting!

I had no Maoist connections in London, so I thought I'd go harass the British commie revisionists who were in love with the Soviet Union. Their little mantra was, "Here's to revolution, but not just yet".

After the boring Communist Party meeting, I arrogantly slammed into them. I told them they sounded like what *we* call "liberal Democrats" in the U.S. I told them it sounded to me as if they were puppets of the Soviet Union, and pointed out Stalin's "excesses", and his betrayal of Marxist-Leninist principles. I harshly criticized *their* revisionist, wimpy Party. I asked, "What about the dictatorship of the proletariat? What about armed struggle?" I grumbled something about, "Revolution isn't sitting in the back room of a public library in Golders Green!" I made my dramatic exit before they could throw me out.

When I returned from London, I became more active in the October League/Communist Party Marxist-Leninist. I attended more meetings and study groups. I read more of the dull, intellectual commie "classics", and even got a tattoo of the Communist Party Marxist-Leninist insignia – a clenched fist holding a hammer and sickle. That would really show the *man* I meant business.

Chapter 40

EDDIE'S SANDBOX

Our family moved from Long Beach when I was a kid, and I had been a resident of Costa Mesa for twenty years, but I still considered Long Beach my hometown. Long Beach was bigger, badder, and blacker than Costa Mesa.

My alcohol and drug binges often started in Costa Mesa and finished in Long Beach, with me exhausted, hungover, and broke. My favorite bar in Long Beach was Eddie's Sandbox.

I discovered Eddie's in the early seventies, and frequented the place often enough to be known and accepted by the owner and a few regular customers.

Eddie's was an African-American bar located on Atlantic Avenue, between Pacific Coast Highway and Willow Street. It was a unique place. Eddie's customers loved to gamble, and many of them smoked reefer. They seemed very open and free about these illegal activities.

I regularly purchased marijuana from one of Eddie's customers. The pot was always Columbian, and it was good weed for those days.

Eddie's Sandbox had rules regarding customer behavior. They were unspoken rules, but I rarely saw them broken. Gambling was O.K. Prostitution was not O.K. Marijuana dealing seemed to be O.K. if done coolly and discretely. Junkies and pushers weren't seen in the bar. Fights and domestic disturbances were forbidden.

Late one Saturday afternoon, I was relaxing at Eddie's. A woman stormed into the bar through the back door. She was brandishing an old long-barreled pump shotgun.

"Where is that sumbitch? Where is that motherfucker?"

In less than a minute, she was disarmed, calmed down, warned, and firmly escorted out of the bar. The shotgun stayed with Eddie. The gentleman she had been looking for was not in the bar.

During my period of white-knuckle sobriety, between 1974 and 1976, I avoided Eddie's Sandbox. I drank soft drinks and fruit juice at the Buccaneer, but I stayed out of Long Beach.

I started drinking so-called non-alcoholic beer in 1975, and discovered I could actually feel a buzz if I chugged two or three cans in quick succession. Years later, I learned there *was* alcohol in near beer – about two percent alcohol – so my buzz was real.

I enjoyed drinking near beer and driving, because I figured I couldn't get arrested for drunk driving, or driving with an open container. I never attempted to conceal my open near beer cans and the six packs in my vehicle.

One day, in late July 1976, I was driving south on the 405 Freeway from Los Angeles to Costa Mesa, drinking my near beer. I was listening to the radio, and heard something on the news I didn't like. I don't remember what it was, but it outraged my pompous, know-it-all, leftist, holier-than-thou, Marxist-Leninist- Mao Tse Tung-thought worldview.

I exited the 405 at Atlantic. Within ten minutes, I was perched on a barstool in Eddie's Sandbox, chugging a *real* beer. That'll show the capitalist imperialist swine! The first iced cold bottle of Budweiser tasted very good after twenty-six months of non-recovery abstinence.

Three Budweisers later, I jumped into my truck and headed back to Costa Mesa – but first, I needed to drive through the nearest Jack-in-the-Box to blow my vegetarianism with a fish sandwich to eat on the way home. I hadn't eaten meat, fish, or eggs in years. All my yogic and political disciplines collapsed like a house of cards soon after taking that first drink.

I didn't tell anyone about my relapse. The following weekend, I consumed several six packs of real beer. Within two weeks, I was back in full swing – beer, vodka, tequila, pot, uppers, and cocaine, a drug I swore I would never use. I stayed drunk and wired on a daily basis for five continuous years. The only days I didn't drink and use were the occasional days and nights the *man* had me in custody for alcohol-related misunderstandings with law enforcement.

Chapter 41

THE PIKE

As a kid growing up in the Long Beach area, the Pike was my favorite place in the whole world!

The Pike was an ancient amusement park located on the beach in downtown Long Beach. In its twentieth century incarnation, the Pike was conceived in 1902, with a huge indoor saltwater bathhouse called, "The Plunge". The Pike was actually born in 1911, with the opening of the Hippodrome Carousel.

The Pike always had a checkered reputation. It was a legitimate tourist attraction, yet it had a dark side. I was intrigued by the dark side of the Pike.

Disneyland, less that an hour away in Anaheim, opened to great fanfare and massive success in the 1950s. I was not the least bit interested in being dragged to Anaheim. I was loyal to the Pike.

As a small child, I remember my parents talking about the Pike. My mom was scared of the place. The Navy Base was nearby, and as World War Two ended, the Pike was a magnet for sailors, prostitutes, and small-time hustlers. The Long Beach Pike was a very exotic place from the 1940s through the 1960s.

I loved to ride all the thrill rides. The Cyclone Racer was a world-class wooden rollercoaster. The Cyclone Racer seemed to demand a human sacrifice every few years.

The Rotor ride was a circular room that spun fast enough to glue a person against the padded wall. Then, the floor dropped out. I loved it!

The Spook House ride actually had a real mummified dead cowboy in it. For years everyone thought it was just a scary-looking dummy until one day when it fell down and broke its real arm.

The Pike had several great shooting galleries. My favorite had real .22 caliber rifles (firing low-powered gallery loads, of course). I spent most of my childhood Pike money at that particular shooting gallery. Imagine, decades of young kids and drunks shooting real rifles at silly little targets, and nobody shot anyone!

One of the few times my dad took me to the Pike, I was about eleven years old. Dad watched me ride all my favorite rides, and afterwards we walked along the midway, checking out all the games-of-chance booths.

Dad tapped me on the shoulder, and directed my attention toward one of the booths.

"Son, do you see the lady running the game over there?"
I replied in the affirmative.

"Well, that's not really a lady. That's a man."
I asked Dad how he could tell. I was shocked and fascinated.

"Note the large hands and the coarse features, son".
I felt like a real grown-up at that moment.

When I returned to California from Nebraska, as an adult, in 1964, my first destination was the Long Beach Pike. As an adult, it was the cocktail bars on or near the midway that attracted me, not the rides, or the shooting galleries, or the games-of-chance. One of my favorite bars on the Pike provided live country music from six in the morning until two o'clock in the morning!

In 1966, two Long Beach policemen literally lifted me off my barstool at a bar called "Hollywood on the Pike". In one fluid movement I was dragged out the door and into the nearest alley for a brief field interrogation. It seemed I matched the description of a Hells Angel they were looking for. I wasn't the person they wanted, but I was flattered they thought I could be a real Hells Angel. The cops ordered me to get on my chopper and "get the hell back to Costa Mesa".

I stayed away from the Pike for about a year. In those days, both the Long Beach Police Department and the Signal Hill Police Department had reputations for being lethally strict in their contact with people who crossed too far over the line.

The Pike had biker bars, Navy bars, Merchant Marine bars, cowboy bars, and bars that had witchy, or even satanic overtones. All this variety was either *on* the Pike itself, or within a few blocks of the Pike.

The Long Beach Pike closed in 1979. Condominiums were built atop the sacred ruins of the Pike. I was deeply saddened.

Chapter 42

INTERNATIONAL WOMEN'S DAY

The Communist Party Marxist-Leninist participated in the big International Women's Day March in San Francisco, the first weekend in March of 1977.

Our Los Angeles region had enough Party members and potential recruits to charter a bus to take us to San Francisco and back to Los Angeles after the weekend's activities.

It was to be a huge event. In addition to middle-of-the-road feminists, lesbians, and anyone interested in equal rights for women, every socialist and communist on the West Coast would be there!

All our rival parties would be represented: The Communist Party USA, revisionist lackeys of the Soviet Union; The Socialist Workers Party; The Progressive Labor Party; the Revolutionary Communist Party (our most powerful Maoist rival); and us, the Communist Party Marxist-Leninist.

We were all supposed to bring our new recruits – "advanced workers" we'd been grooming in our factory organizing missions. I brought a drinking buddy from my Buccaneer Bar days. We pretended he was an "advanced worker".

Our group was scheduled to depart East Los Angeles in our chartered bus. When my advanced worker and I arrived in East L.A. we found a beat-up old school bus waiting for us. I thought to myself, "We're going to ride eight hundred miles round trip in this piece-of-shit school bus? Commies!

We boarded the bus, and headed north on the 5 Freeway. The cadre leaders made us sing communist songs until I wanted to scream, "Shut the fuck up!" Don't get me wrong, I love the *Internationale,* sung in English, Spanish, and Chinese, as much as the next guy, but it got old after a while.

The bus broke down at Buttonwillow, near Bakersfield. We sat on the freeway for hours – not singing – thank God. I was craving a drink. Maybe I could hitch a ride into Bakersfield, where there were many bars, and lots of Buck Owens music on the jukeboxes.

What was I doing with these revolutionaries who just seemed to endlessly discuss, and talk, and hold meetings, and engage in intense criticism/self-criticism sessions? I wanted to "build a new world from the ashes of the old". Heavy on the "ashes of the old" part.

When the bus was finally fixed, it took us nearly ten more hours to cough and chug our way into the city of San Francisco.

My advanced worker and I, during the bus ride from hell, secretly decided we were going to bug out and hit a few bars in the City, before the big march.

When we arrived at our assembly point in the Mission District, it was already the morning of the big parade. We hadn't slept, and I was very thirsty and cranky.

Things became kind of blurry after that. So many bars, all within walking distance! We completely avoided the parade route.

As I remember, we took a cab to San Francisco International Airport. Plane tickets were purchased with a credit card that didn't belong to us. More drinks on the airplane. Arrival at Orange County

Airport, and the simultaneous realization that my truck was still in East Los Angeles. We called another Buckaroo from a payphone at the airport, and he gave me a ride to pick up my truck.

Several days later, I received a phone call from my cadre leader, ordering me to meet him and a few other comrades at a coffee shop in Long Beach. I knew I was in trouble with the Party, but didn't care. The members of the Communist Party Marxist-Leninist I had met were dedicated, sincere, focused, and very principled in their own way. Their lack of humor, and their unwillingness to even consider there was anything beyond the physical universe was boring and irritating to me.

I met the comrades at the appointed place and time. They ordered me to self-criticize my behavior in San Francisco. I told them I was "guilty of bourgeois self-interest, rightist opportunism, and of bowing to spontaneity."

They agreed, expanded upon my self-criticism, and told me to return to the Party when I was seriously committed to the struggle. I think they were so easy on me because I was, unlike many of them, a real working-class proletarian with working-class roots. My infantry training may have been a consideration as well.

I thanked them for investing their time and energy in me, and apologized for being such a loose cannon. I never saw any of my old comrades again.

Chapter 43

ROUTE DRIVER

From 1977 to 1979, I drove a delivery van from North Long Beach to Paso Robles and back every day. I delivered photographic equipment, film, and photos from a large photo lab in Paramount, California, to camera stores along my route.

The round trip run took up to fourteen hours. I made stops in Lompoc, Santa Maria, Arroyo Grande, San Luis Obispo, Morro Bay, Atascadero, and Paso Robles. It was a Teamsters Union job, and the overtime was great. Long hours, alone on the road, were boring and tiring. Within a few months, I was amusing myself by looking through the customers' photos while driving – searching for homegrown porno. I found some, too! I became familiar with certain customers' names on the labels. They were usually the hot ones. Amateur home porno was much better than professional, because the folks were really into it, and looked like they were having fun. I also drank constantly, and popped uppers like candy while I drove – and I drove very fast.

When I returned to North Long Beach each night, I parked the van in the company parking lot, and threw away all the empty alcohol containers. I had the longest route and was the last driver to arrive back at the lab each night. This worked out well because there was no one around to see how drunk and wired I was at the end of my shift. After cleaning out the company van, I'd hop into my trusty 1964 El Camino, named "Buck", and make the one-hour drive home to Costa Mesa. The same routine started again at five-thirty the following morning.

After almost two years of this grind, I burned out and cracked up. One morning, I rolled out of North Long Beach, northbound on the 405, buzzed and wired as usual. The company van was fully loaded, and I had a pretty good start myself.

Many miles short of my first stop, the vehicle exited the 101 Freeway in Oxnard, California. I observed the van parking itself in front of a Mexican bar called the "Roadrunner". It was nine in the morning. The bar was open. I supposed I better go in and have a shot of tequila or something, since I was there.

When I drank, my barroom Spanish bordered on fluency, and by about three in the afternoon, I was holding forth in Spanish. *"Raza, Si! Migra, No!" "Viva Emiliano Zapata!"* I also shouted something about "The Treaty of Guadalupe Hidalgo".

I mumbled into my tequila shot glass, "I need to be north of Santa Barbara by noon". An old Mexican farm worker reminded me I wasn't going to make it on time. I laughed. "Come with me, *Hermano*, I'll show you something funny".

We went out into the parking lot. I told my new best friend to stand clear. I faced the threatening company van, eyeball to headlight. I drew a revolver from my waistband, and emptied all six rounds into the radiator of the deadly beast. "Well, that settles it. I'm stuck here!" Laughing heartily in Spanish, we returned to the bar.

Around midnight, I called Jerry, in Costa Mesa, and explained my situation. Without a word of complaint, my good friend drove all the way up to Oxnard in the middle of the night. At my insistence, he even let me drive home, so he could rest.

149

The next morning I awoke in a cold sweat. "Oh my God, what have I done?" I called the lab, told them the van broke down in Oxnard, and suggested they should go ahead and terminate me immediately.

I assumed I was having a nervous breakdown and better go see a doctor. I was in total denial that alcohol and other drugs had anything to do with my acting out. The revolver was just something I usually had close at hand, but I normally carried it in my black metal, real workingman's lunch pail. In true alcoholic grandiosity, I thought, "I'm a Red and a Teamsters Union Member. I should be armed at all times. You never know when the neo-nazis, agents of the Nationalist Chinese Kuomintang, or even the mysterious Omega-7, would want to neutralize an important worker such as myself!

I made an appointment to see a doctor at a small clinic in Long Beach. He took one look at me and picked up the phone. "I've got a man in my office under extreme stress. You need to see him right now!" The doctor didn't listen to my heart, weigh me, or take my blood pressure. He just handed me a card and said, "Go see him immediately. You'll like him". I looked at the name on the card. The man was obviously from India and was a psychiatrist.

The psychiatrist's office was just a few blocks away, in the same hospital complex where my brother was born in 1948, and my dad died in 1973. I walked into the waiting room, filled out some forms and sat down. I was very scared and anxious. The doctor popped out of his office, glanced at me and said, "Hi!" He scribbled something on a pad, and handed me a prescription for Valium. The doctor told me to have the prescription filled downstairs at the pharmacy, go straight home and take the Valium as directed. "Come back in three days – eleven in the morning. I'll have time to see you then. Don't leave your home until it's time to come here!"

I followed his advice to the letter. Three days later, at eleven in the morning, I showed up for a real psychiatric session. The doctor at the clinic was right. I liked this Indian psychiatrist.

In the session, we verified the fact I acted out on the job and destroyed company property. The revolver was not mentioned.

We discussed the transitory and illusionary nature of what we call "reality". We agreed that at the time of death, we cannot take any of our so-called possessions or our worldly attachments with us. We agreed there is a Higher Power, and it made sense to attach ourselves to that unchanging Power. I told the psychiatrist I believed in karma and reincarnation, and wanted to get off the wheel of birth and death. I also disclosed I had experienced glimpses of what I believe to have been past lives.

The session lasted one full hour. The doctor summed it up with these exact words: "Marc, you do not need a psychiatrist; what you need is a meaningful job." He suggested I go back to school and become a counselor or therapist. He said, "You need a piece of paper."

The psychiatrist put me on three months of disability, and I never saw him again. I didn't get clean and sober until several years later, but I'll never forget him. He was the first " professional" person in my life who validated me for having potential for doing good.

Chapter 44

THE APACHE

It was absolutely necessary to find a job as soon as my disability expired. I knew I could never get another driver job. My little meltdown in Oxnard would surely come to light in any employment background check.

I decided to sneak back into the aerospace industry, and got hired as a Quality Control Inspector in a small machine shop in South Gate. I covered-up my last two years as a driver by claiming I'd been "self-employed, trimming doors for independent carpet layers." Jerry and I *had* done that for several weeks in our Buckaroo days. We called ourselves *Aquarius Lawn Service and Pitiful Chores*. It didn't work out too well at the time. We screwed up almost every job that came our way.

My new employer manufactured precision springs used by large aerospace companies in the manufacture of aircraft, missiles, and diving equipment.

I was less than the ideal employee, due to my daily consumption of beverage alcohol and upper drugs. My usual payday routine was to cash my check during lunch break, and hit as many bars as I could on the way home. My route was systematic. I'd start in East Los Angeles, on Atlantic Avenue, and work my way down Atlantic to Pacific Coast Highway in Long Beach. To avoid confusion, I would only stop at bars on the right-hand side of the street. When I finally arrived at Pacific Coast Highway, I'd point the nose of the El Camino south, and one hour later I would be passed out at home in Costa Mesa.

Occasionally, I would deviate from my normal route, and drive around Lynwood or Compton, looking for interesting bars. One bar really fascinated me, but it took months of driving past it before I could work up the courage to enter the place.

The Apache was the only business still standing, in a burned-out strip mall in Compton. From the look of the abandoned structural remains adjacent to the Apache, I figured the strip mall had been destroyed during the Watts Riots. The Apache literally radiated menace. I had been in many nasty bars in my twenty years of hard drinking, but the Apache felt especially dangerous.

One night, after work, I drove up to Hollywood from my job in the spring factory. I scored a "six weeks" supply of uppers and a B12 shot from my speed clinic on Sunset. By the time I entered the southbound Long Beach Freeway, I was really drunk and wired. "Tonight's the night for the Apache!"

I stopped at several bars between Hollywood and Compton. By the time I pulled into the chuck-hole permeated parking lot of the Apache, it was one in the morning, and I was feeling wild and self-destructive. I parked the El Camino in front of the bar and just sat behind the steering wheel for several minutes, observing the area. A few cars were parked haphazardly in the mostly unpaved parking lot. No functional streetlights were visible. The parking lot was deserted of living human beings, but I could sense the ghosts of the past. I felt I had entered a lower astral region. A tumbleweed blew across the parking lot to emphasize the weirdness of the experience.

A wooden Indian stood guard in front of the bar. I had never noticed it previously, even though I'd driven past the Apache many times in the daylight hours.

I popped two more uppers and washed them down with one of the bottles of pre-mixed Zombies I'd purchased at a liquor store near Sunset and La Brea earlier in the evening.

I took a Complete Yogic Breath, got out of the El Camino, locked it, and headed for the front door of the Apache Bar. I was unarmed. Part of me wanted to live; part of me didn't care.

The front door of the bar was open, but a thick, red velvet curtain hung in the doorway. I needed to pull aside the curtain to actually enter the bar.

I parted the curtain and stepped inside. The horseshoe-shaped bar was completely full of customers. I was surprised, because there were so few cars outside.

I had to make a very quick decision -- either turn around, run for my El Camino and get the hell out of Compton, or balls it out.

Since I had everyone's undivided attention, I decided to go for it. As we all know, even a small amount of alcohol impairs judgment and lowers inhibitions.

"Hey!" I shouted. "I heard this motherfucker was tough!"

A stunned silence followed. Then everyone cracked up. They *knew* I figured I was as good as dead, anyway, so why not take it over the top?

Someone moved over and pointed to an empty barstool. I thanked the people to my left and right for accepting me, and ordered a tall glass of tequila and grapefruit juice. I think they called it a "tequila greyhound".

Before I could finish my drink, I felt the energy in the room change. The hostility was building again.

"Don't press your luck, Marc", came that voice in my head. I gulped down the rest of my drink and made a gracious, respectful exit from the Apache Bar. I knew I didn't need to experience that place again. It wasn't what I was really looking for. I think I just wanted someone to put me out of my misery, but my life urges were a little stronger than I had anticipated.

Chapter 45

HIT AND RUN, PROPERTY

I generally enjoyed taking the scenic route home from my adventures in East Los Angeles. This particular night I was doing my, "I'll-stop-at-bars-on-the-right-hand-side-of-Atlantic Avenue routine.

I started my run in South Gate and was headed home to Costa Mesa via Long Beach. Around two-thirty in the morning, I ran a red light near Atlantic and Ocean, and was broad-sided by another car traveling at high speed.

I remember sitting calmly behind the steering wheel as the interior of my El Camino started raining glass particles. The vehicle spun like a pinwheel. Everything really did seem to be happening in slow motion, just the way people describe the experience. I always thought those descriptions were over-dramatic.

When the El Camino stopped spinning, I brushed the glass off myself, and tried to re-start the engine. The little 327 Chevy started right up!

The sentence, "I wonder if the porno theater downtown is still open at this time of night?" went through my mind. I simultaneously realized I wasn't wearing my glasses. No wonder everything looked so blurry. My glasses must have flown off during the impact, when my head broke the driver's side window.

"Well", I thought, "I'll just drive away from this downtown intersection and park in a residential area nearby while I look for my glasses".

I drove away from the scene of the crash and parked in a quiet neighborhood, several blocks east of Atlantic.

I was crawling around the floor of my wrecked El Camino, feeling around for my glasses, when I was distracted by sirens and flashing lights. Two Long Beach cops pulled me out of my vehicle and asked me what the hell I was doing. I told them I was looking for my glasses. "You won't need glasses where you're going", was their somewhat cryptic reply.

The officers asked me if I had any weapons on me. I said I didn't. During the "pat down", they found my Buck knife tucked into the secret thigh pocket of my overalls. The cops became very angry, and slammed me against the hood of the police car.

"We're taking you to Signal Hill, motherfucker. You shouldn't have lied to us."

They handcuffed me and placed me in the *front* passenger seat. One cop slid in behind the steering wheel; the other disappeared into one of the back-up units on the scene.

Sure enough, we headed toward Signal Hill. I became sober enough to feel some fear. Signal Hill, California had its own Police Department. That department had been rocked with scandal over the previous several years. A number of suspicious deaths of prisoners who had displayed unacceptable attitudes, had brought media attention to Signal Hill.

I assumed they were going to take me up there and beat me up for lying to them about the Buck knife. I told the officer who was driving, that I had forgotten I had the knife in my possession. He wasn't in a mood to believe me.

When I was a kid, growing up in Lakewood, one of my childhood friends had become a Long Beach cop. After mentally going through the alphabet, I remembered his name. I asked my "driver" if he knew him. He grunted, and flipped a U-turn on Pacific Coast Highway – at the foot of Signal Hill.

The cops booked me into the Long Beach City Jail. I refused to take a blood alcohol test, so that was an automatic suspension of my driver's license under California's "Implied Consent" law. I was charged with first offense drunk driving and hit and run, property. My Buck knife and several envelopes containing pharmaceutical upper drugs were confiscated.

I called my significant other, in Costa Mesa, and asked her to please bring my extra pair of glasses. I told her I was in the Long Beach City Jail, and I was unable to see, due to my extreme nearsightedness. I tried to communicate to her the fact I needed to be able to see, to protect myself in the jail.

She almost paraphrased the police officer's earlier remark to me. She said, "You don't need to see in there; the walls are close enough together."

I told my cell-mates what she had said. They were shocked. "That's cold, man. That's *cold*! They felt sorry for me, I guess, because they kept a protective eye on me during my short stay in the Long Beach City Jail.

Within a few days, I was released on my own recognizance. My Buck knife and uppers were returned to me.

When I went to court, I was given a large fine, a one- year suspension of my driver's license, over and above the "Implied

Consent" suspension, and I was ordered to make restitution to the other driver.

Chapter 46

MACHINE GUN BOY

Christmas morning, 1980.

Someone living in or near my apartment complex called the Costa Mesa Police Department. It was reported that a man matching my description had fired an automatic rifle into the air after yelling, "Fuck Christmas!"

At the same time, and in the same neighborhood, I was hurriedly stowing my Ruger Mini-14 semi-automatic rifle, my twelve-gauge riot gun, several spare thirty-round magazines, and five boxes of shotgun slugs into the trunk of my car.

I jumped into my vehicle and headed north on Pacific Coast Highway. My poor El Camino was no more, and I was driving an old Plymouth someone had loaned me. The one-hour drive to Long Beach was uneventful. No lights. No sirens. My driver's license had been suspended about eight months previously because of my traffic collision, hit-and-run, property, and drunk driving misunderstanding in downtown Long Beach.

My previous DUI and the very intense encounter with the Long Beach Police and their scary jail, hadn't stopped me from driving, license or no license. I paid my fine, made what financial restitution I was capable of making, and felt squared-away in the karmic sense of the word. I didn't need a scrap of paper from the *man* telling me I could drive!

I rented a motel room on the Long Beach/Wilmington border and took a little vacation. I drank in familiar bars in Long Beach, and killed cockroaches in my motel room.

One week later I was down to my last ten dollars. I called several friends in Costa Mesa, to check on the situation. I was informed the police wanted to arrest me for "firing a machine gun on Christmas morning!" I decided to go home anyway. It was January 2, 1981 – a brand new year. Maybe it would all go away.

I stopped in Huntington Beach on the way back to Costa Mesa, and dropped off the rifle and shotgun at a co-worker's house. I told him what was going on, and we agreed I shouldn't drive into Costa Mesa bristling with firearms.

I arrived at Dick's Horseshoe Saloon around nine in the morning, parked in the lot behind the bar, and went inside for a drink. I still had my ten dollars and I deserved a snort or two to relieve my stress. I was working on my fourth tequila and grapefruit juice, when a uniformed Costa Mesa cop walked through the bar- in one door and out the other. My highly developed yogic intuition told me the officer was looking for me. I stage-whispered proudly to the other guys at the bar, "They're after *me*. I gotta go!" Nobody looked up from their drinks, or seemed to give a shit.

I got into my borrowed car and slowly pulled out of Dick's parking lot. My goal was to take residential streets home, and go hide in bed. I lived about two miles from Dick's Horseshoe Saloon. From my rearview mirror, I noticed a red sub-compact car following me. I turned left, they turned left. They looked like two guys I'd seen in the bar several minutes earlier. I turned right, they turned right. I suddenly got a sinking feeling in my stomach. I turned left, and there were police cars everywhere. The street was completely blocked. The two guys from the little red sub-compact ran up to my car, pistols drawn. I noticed one officer was pointing a .380 Auto at me. I thought, ".380 must be the minimum caliber allowed for Costa Mesa plainclothes officers".

My driver's side door flew open, and the next thing I remember is my nose hitting the hard surface of the street. "What's the karma with my nose and the street all the time?" flashed through my mind.

Face down, in the middle of a residential street, I experienced everything in slow motion one more time. The cops handcuffed my arms behind my back with just the appropriate amount of force for the situation. The muzzles of the .380 Auto *and* a police shotgun were pointed at my head.

I couldn't help but notice the officer's shotgun was a very cool Remington 870 with an extended high-capacity magazine. It was superior to my ported Mossberg 500, with it's standard length magazine, eighteen and one-half inch barrel, and pistol grip. I made a mental note to buy an 870 in the near future.

Neighborhood residents were gawking out their windows and standing in their doorways. I enjoyed the attention. Four Dick's Horseshoe-sized drinks in less than an hour had sedated the part of my mind that could feel shame. I was having a great time!

"Where's the machine gun?" the officers kept yelling at me. I took the attention off my dramatic self for a moment and noticed the police had thoroughly searched my car looking for this alleged "machine gun". I didn't answer. The cops helped me to my feet. I stood proudly, hands cuffed behind my back; my slightly bloodied nose a silent testimony to the world that I may be another victim of police brutality.

The officers placed me in the back seat of one of the police cars, and we all convoyed the few remaining blocks to my apartment.

Once inside my apartment, the police began searching the place. They were making a real mess. One of the undercover officers said, "We've already got you on Second Offense Drunk Driving, and Driving on a Suspended License. If you don't turn in that rifle, or carbine, or machine gun, or whatever it is, we'll make your life really miserable".

I picked up the phone, called my friend in Huntington Beach, told him I was in custody and the Costa Mesa Police Department needed to examine the guns I'd left with him for safe-keeping. I asked him to bring them to the police station as soon as possible.

We all left my apartment, and I was booked into the Costa Mesa Jail. After initial booking, I was transported, handcuffed and at gunpoint, to a local hospital. I hadn't co-operated with the breath or urine tests, so they had to take me to a hospital in order to draw blood. I was informed later my blood alcohol level was over twice the legal limit for a drunk driving charge.

On the way to the hospital, I heard police radio chatter. "Did anybody get Machine Gun Boy?" The officer driving me to the hospital replied, "Yeah, I've got him here with me". I thought Machine Gun Boy was a very cool name!

My co-worker brought my guns into the police station. The police firearms experts examined the weapons and returned them to me when I was released on bail several days later.

My firearms *were* legal and could not be fired in a fully-automatic mode. I was either not Machine Gun Boy, or I emptied a thirty-round magazine so fast (muzzle pointed harmlessly toward the ocean) that it *sounded* like a machine gun.

Chapter 47

ORANGE COUNTY JAIL

My lawyer was a great guy – codependent – but a great guy. On my court date he escorted me from courtroom to courtroom until he found the most liberal judge in the building. I was to plead guilty to second offense drunk driving, and the *man* would drop the other charges. The "Machine Gun Boy" misunderstanding would be forgotten. I thought it was a very good deal.

The judge offered me one year of Alcoholics Anonymous meetings on a court card and one year of alcohol counseling – one session per week. I would be given credit for time served in the Costa Mesa Jail. I would be allowed to drive to and from work, to my AA meetings, and to my counseling sessions. Any other driving would be considered a violation of this very generous and lenient agreement.

I refused the offer. I rejected Alcoholics Anonymous because I had heard it was some kind of Jesus freak cult. I refused counseling, because "counseling" meant there was something wrong with me psychologically. I refused to stop drinking.

The judge was a little irritated by my decision, but he was doing his best to prevent me from experiencing the full consequences of my irresponsible, destructive and anti-social behavior. He offered me weekends at a minimum security facility.

This meant serving ten weekends, and suspension of my driver's license for another year. I thought weekends in jail were for punks, so I refused that offer as well.

The good judge said, "That's it", and sentenced me to a few days less than one month in Orange County Main Jail, suspension of my driver's license, and a very large fine. My lawyer just shook his head in disbelief.

I was not deemed a flight risk, so I was allowed to go home, go back to work, organize my life, and check myself into Orange County Jail within two weeks.

My employer allowed me to combine my two weeks vacation with the several days of sick leave I still had coming. That would just about do it.

Immediately before checking into the jail, I consumed a large pitcher of Margaritas at my favorite Mexican restaurant in Santa Ana. The intake process was pretty fuzzy. I was asked if I had any tattoos or distinguishing marks. I said, "No". When I was stripped for delousing and shower, I prayed they wouldn't see the Communist Party Marxist-Leninist tattoo above my left ankle.

I was then offered a reduction in my sentence if I would shave off my long beard, and cut my hair. I refused, of course!

At that time (April 1981), Orange County Main Jail had a policy on long hair and beards. Inmates who submitted to haircuts and clean-shaven faces generally received some time knocked off their sentences. Those who complied also received dayroom, commissary and television privileges. These inmates wore orange jumpsuits. They also showered regularly and received exercise periods on the roof.

Those of us who refused to shave and cut our hair were segregated to the "soup tank", a tier of four-man cells located directly across from the large, spacious group cells the normal population called "home". We were issued black sweatshirts with "Orange County Men's Jail" stenciled in white letters. We were also issued blue jeans instead of jumpsuits. I really liked the look!

I remember only one shower per week and one trip to the roof for exercise. We had no dayroom privileges, no television viewing, no pencils, paper, or commissary treats, such as candy bars or peanuts. I received no visitors.

The three other men in my cell were all convicted felons; an outlaw biker, convicted of strong-arm robbery, a habitual car thief, and a heroin dealer. The heroin dealer told me he had occupied the same cell for one year, awaiting further disposition of his case. Justice was slow for him, but he was very mellow about it. The only time I saw him upset was when Jeff, the young car thief, woke him up unexpectedly.

Jeff was a product of the California Youth Authority. He had now graduated to the adult criminal justice system. Orange County Jail was full of guys like Jeff. They knew each other from the C.Y.A. system, and had longtime jailhouse relationships with each other. Everyone was called, "Homey", or "Es-Say'!" or "Punk", or "Bitch". Jeff had lots of enemies, and he got roughed-up on a regular basis. When our cell door was opened to let us out for our meals, Jeff's former associates would rush in and pop him a few times upside his head. It seemed harmless enough, considering Jeff's irritating, obnoxious behavior.

The biker was a quiet man, covered with tattoos. He passed his time doing push-ups between the double bunks.

At night, I could clearly hear prisoner-on-prisoner violence. It was very scary. Movies portray it, but you have to be there to feel the horrible vibes.

The occupants of the eight, four-man cells in the "soup tank" had a little ritual. I didn't participate out of fear of retaliation. Whenever the general population filed out of their luxurious cells to go to the dayroom, the soup tank guys would yell at them, "Dayroom makes you weak! TV makes you weak!" Of course, they'd yell back threats on our lives.

Jeff was very easily influenced. One day, some of his old California Youth Authority buddies shouted at him to, "Do Bojangles, Jeff. Do Bojangles!" The deputies yelled at everyone to shut up, but Jeff went to the front of the cell, grabbed the bars, and started singing *Mister Bojangles*. He even tried to tap dance in his jail shower shoes. We were hysterical! The other inmates goaded him on. "You still got it, Jeff! You still got it!"

Naturally, the deputies rushed in and dragged Jeff out, still singing *Mister Bojangles*. They threw him into isolation for a day or two. It was nice and quiet in our cell without him. We were grown-ups.

I essentially went on a long fast during my time in the Orange County Jail. The first week, I stayed in my cell, and sat in a half-lotus position, trying to meditate while everyone was in the mess hall. One day a, deputy came into my cell and asked me if I was O.K. I told him I just wasn't hungry. I didn't tell him I was fasting, because I was afraid they'd think I was a troublemaker.

I had only served about half my little sentence when I was mysteriously released. I have no idea why, but around two in the morning, my cell door was electronically opened, and the deputy told me to grab my stuff. I was processing out. I didn't ask questions.

At five-thirty in the morning, I had finished the long out-processing, and I needed to use the restroom in the reception area.

When I was in the restroom, another just-released inmate came in. He was a clean-cut white guy about my age. We didn't speak to each other, but the pure evil radiating off him was so strong I could almost see it. It almost knocked me over.

Prior to this jail experience, I believed the majority of incarcerated people were victims of racism or capitalism. Now, I believe some souls are just evil – consciously evil.

By six in the morning, I was sitting on a barstool in downtown Santa Ana, drinking tequila, beating my chest, and bragging about surviving the horrors of Orange County Main Jail.

Chapter 48

HITTING BOTTOM

The Orange County Jail experience took place during the spring of 1981. Upon my release, I was definitely scared-straight as far as not drinking and driving, and not driving with a suspended driver's license.

I now drank and walked, or drank and took the bus, or drank and rode with friends. My alcohol and drug use escalated, and my performance on the job dropped to a new low.

Amazingly, I had held the same job for over three years. I left the spring factory, in the East Los Angeles area, under a dark alcoholic cloud of absenteeism, tardiness, and sloppy work. Somehow, I bull-shitted my way into a new job in Santa Ana, a factory much closer to home.

I worked as a Quality Control Inspector in a mid-sized aerospace company. We manufactured precision steel bearings for the giant aerospace companies.

I still lived in Machine Gun Boy's apartment complex in Costa Mesa. I walked six miles to work every morning, and took the bus home after work every evening. My driver's license was still suspended, of course.

I arose at four in the morning every workday, and began my little ritual. I showered, dressed (overalls, T-shirt, and boots), and stumbled into the kitchen. I prepared a big mug of instant coffee, added one teaspoon of honey, three eyedroppers full of concentrated Chinese ginseng, and two shots of Cuervo Gold tequila. With this potion, I washed down two capsules of stress B-complex and three pharmaceutical grade uppers. I popped a gram of hashish and half a Hershey bar into my mouth as I walked out my apartment door. I chewed this hash-chocolate treat on my way to work.

I left my apartment at four-thirty in the morning. The six-mile walk to Santa Ana took me a leisurely one and one-half hours. I stopped to smell the flowers and maybe smoke a joint along the way. By the time I arrived in Santa Ana, I was buzzed, dry-mouthed and very thirsty. Six miles of deep yogic breathing, combined with the drugs and alcohol put me in a very unusual state of consciousness.

My timing was perfect. The liquor store on the corner of Fairview and Warner, near the factory, opened at six in the morning. The factory doors opened at six-thirty and my shift started at seven in the morning.

As soon as the liquor store opened, I bought a pint, and a half-pint of vodka, a quart of orange juice, and a half-gallon plastic container of bottled water.

I'd carry this big bag of groceries to the factory parking lot, where I would pour out the water and pour in the vodka and orange juice. I bought a pint, and a half-pint because I thought a fifth of vodka would be excessive – although cheaper. I didn't want to think of myself as a lush. A fifth a day on the job-- *alcoholics* did that!

As soon as I entered the factory, I placed the jug in a sub-zero freezer used to freeze metals during part of the heat-treating process. Within a few minutes, my big vodka and orange juice was frozen solid. I took my now-frozen jug to my workbench, where I'd nip on it all day as it thawed to a refreshing, slushy drink. The factory was not air conditioned and was always hot, smelly, and uncomfortable.

Often, my work consisted of inspecting an endless supply of two-inch steel spherical bearings, to tolerances of plus or minus two-tenths of a *thousandth* of an inch. Some days I sat at my workbench for hours, not talking, not walking around, inspecting spherical bearings and drinking vodka and orange juice. I tried not to breathe on anyone!

We had a one-half hour lunch break. I'd usually catch a ride with another drunk to the nearest bar. We'd split a joint on the two-block ride.

Paddy Murphy's, the bar nearest to the factory, was a blue collar Santa Ana topless bar. I drank my lunch there every workday, and cashed my paycheck there every week. The moment I walked through the door, the bartender had two tequila grapefruit drinks on the bar. I was as regular as a clock, because I only had twenty actual minutes to sit on the barstool and enjoy my lunch.

After work, I always rode the bus home, or to the last home-bar of my drinking career, Dick's Horseshoe Saloon in Costa Mesa.

I was able to maintain this rigorous daily schedule of suicidal substance abuse for eight months. Of course on weekends I drank and used much more than the amount I rationed myself for the workweek.

The evening of December 18, 1981, was just another night of drinking at Dick's. It was Friday night. I'd completed another workweek at the factory and I deserved to kick back with my *real* family at Dick's Horseshoe Saloon! Spouses, secondary significant others, and blood relatives were hassles that had to be temporarily endured out of obligation. Our real families were our drinking buddies.

I played all my favorite songs on the jukebox. As usual, *I Can Still Hear The Music In The Restroom*, by Jerry Lee Lewis, was number one on my parade of hits. That song captured the essence of the barroom alcoholic. I played it every time I went to Dick's Horseshoe.

As two in the morning approached, the bartender yelled, "Last call for alcohol!" He flashed the lights off and on to emphasize the point.

I ordered one more drink, consumed it, and caught a ride home with some drinking buddies. As they dropped me off at my apartment, I remember agreeing to go to Jerry's wife's birthday party the next day.

The morning of December 19th, I awoke in a cold sweat. I got out of bed and sat in my chair. I felt I was freaking out. Then, a moment of clarity. I saw myself as I really was. I was outside my body looking at myself, a thirty-nine year old man dying of alcoholism. I had never used the word, "alcoholic" to describe myself. On the rare occasion when someone confronted me about my drinking, I would say, "I like to drink", and glare at them to make them stop.

The experience I had that morning was profound. Images and memories flooded into my consciousness. My entire alcohol and drug history was revealed to me with absolute clarity.

I got drunk and deathly ill on homemade wine at age sixteen. I even drank the grape residue at the bottom of the jug.

I ran off the road and hit a bulldozer on the South Dakota/Nebraska border at age nineteen.

I emerged from a blackout in a scary apartment building in Harlem in the middle of the night when I was in the Army. I couldn't remember how I got to Harlem.

I thought about all the commitments I had broken, the relationships I had destroyed, the many good people I had taken advantage of.

I remembered how, over the years, my personality had changed from the mellow, cheerful guy everyone was happy to see, to the volatile, unpredictable, violent drunk.

I remembered all the times and all the methods I used in my vain attempts to limit my drinking, or to quit drinking altogether.

Pot and acid were my drugs of choice when I first became a hippie because I believed they were mind-expanding "sacraments". Alcohol, on the other hand, was the drug the *man* took to numb-out his guilty conscience for his exploitation of the oppressed masses.

Many hippies looked upon drinkers as "juice heads". The hippies were, after all, seekers of Truth, Universal Peace and Unconditional Love.

This anti-alcohol philosophy hadn't stuck with me. In my hippie days, I craved avocados, chips, cheese, and numerous pitchers of ice cold beer to quench my marijuana munchies. I ran to the vodka or tequila bottles whenever I experienced psychedelic bummers.

I periodically fasted to detoxify my body. If I was able to get through the third day of a fast, my hunger and cravings would subside. The longest fast I endured was twenty-one days on distilled water and herbal tea. After each fast, I resumed drinking alcohol immediately.

I went to monasteries and spiritual retreats, but all I could think about was getting back to my friends at the Buccaneer, or Dick's Horseshoe Saloon.

I remembered the two years and two months I had completely abstained from alcohol and other drugs. From May 25,

1974 through July of 1976, I had followed a very pure spiritual path on one hand and a highly disciplined revolutionary political life on the other.

The spiritual path of yoga I followed, included maintaining a strict lacto-vegetarian diet and meditating as prescribed by a living Saint in the Punjab of India. I meditated two and one-half hours a day, from three to five-thirty every morning.

At the same time I was truly living a double life. I kept my spiritual life a secret from my revolutionary comrades. They disapproved of all things spiritual, but they tolerated my vegetarianism. This was, after all, Los Angeles!

The relapse, which followed my two years of white-knuckle abstinence, lasted five long years. A descent into "incomprehensible demoralization" truly describes it.

The realization finally permeated every cell of my body, and every corner of my mind, that *my* best efforts could not keep me sober. My denial was gone. Alcohol and other drugs had completely defeated me.

I humbly asked a Power greater than myself to take over. I didn't "think" in words. It was more like a perception of the Master's Grace coming into my life.

I grabbed a legal pad and started writing. I wrote all that morning and into the afternoon. I wrote about all the hurtful things I had done over the past twenty-two years of drinking and using. I wrote about my gross acting-out, my destruction of other people's property, and my manipulation of people to further my own agendas. It was awful!

When I finished this searching and fearless moral inventory of myself, I felt lighter and freer than I could ever remember.

I picked up the phone. My first call was to a former female drinking buddy from my Buccaneer Bar days. We referred to female Buckaroos as "Buckareens"! I'd heard she "got religion", and was working with alcoholics. When I told her what I was experiencing, she suggested I call a man at her church who was an expert in the field of alcoholism.

I called the expert. He asked me only one question. "Where did you drink?" I told him I drank at Dick's Horseshoe. He gave me a phone number and said, "Call these folks. You belong with them."

At this point, I was willing to go to any lengths. I called the number. It was the Orange County Central Office of a twelve-step program. The man at Central Office told me there was an "Open Speaker Meeting", being held the following evening within walking distance of my apartment. He also suggested I go to a meeting immediately. I knew he was right but I needed sleep. I felt relieved to know the fight was over. I'd been running from this Program for years.

I didn't leave my apartment until it was time to go to my meeting. I had to walk right past Dick's Horseshoe Saloon to get there. I didn't even notice Dick's. I was so focused on getting to my first meeting. I was nervous and excited, and I felt very hopeful. I could not remember the last time I felt hopeful.

I sat quietly in the room during the meeting. I didn't identify myself or raise my hand as a newcomer.

The Speaker told *my* story. It was more than eerie! As I looked around the room, I saw the Twelve Steps on the wall. Although I'd never seen them before, I realized I'd been working the first four steps over the last two days without even knowing it.

More memories flooded into my mind during the meeting. I remembered sitting, scared out of my wits, in Orange County Main

Jail seven months previously. I was in that jail because I had arrogantly refused the judge's offer of Alcoholics Anonymous and alcoholism counseling in lieu of jail time. In my denial and shame, I had tried to convince myself the program was a religious cult. Nothing could have been farther from the truth. I had known absolutely nothing about alcoholism or recovery.

Now, I saw things differently. I knew I belonged in that room and in rooms just like it all over the world. I was home.

Chapter 49

RECOVERY

Recovery from alcoholism opened up a new world and a new life. I attended my 12 Step meetings, went to work every day and stayed out of the bars. I had to avoid the Buckaroos and my "family" at Dick's Horseshoe Saloon. Meetings were a new experience for me. I listened carefully to the old-timers, but had little to share myself. I attended many *different* meetings in the Orange County/Long Beach area, because I didn't want anyone to get too close to my shame and pain. The same message was broadcast in all the meetings: "Keep Coming Back; It Works if You Work It, It Don't if You Don't! Work the Steps or Die. Get a Sponsor. Stay Out of Slippery Places. Don't Get Into Any New Relationships For a Year."

The compulsion to drink and use had been lifted, but I knew I had to do my part to remain sober. I eventually made a list of persons I'd harmed during my twenty years of drinking and drugging. The people I'd hurt the most were at the top of the list. I set about trying to make amends to them all. This Step contains a common-sense loophole. A person isn't supposed to make direct amends to someone if contacting that person would injure them or others. I had to be careful. I paid back money to people I owed, apologized to people I'd hurt, and generally tried to square things the best I could. Some folks accepted my apologies gracefully, a few wouldn't accept my amends, and several didn't know what the hell I was talking about.

I called two former significant others, gave them my most heartfelt apologies for the misery I'd put them through with my drinking and using. I asked them if there was anything I could do to make amends. The woman I'd been with the longest, and put through the worst experiences, was most gracious and forgiving. She told me she was really glad I was in recovery, had always worried about me, and said, "It took both of us to create such a dysfunctional relationship." The second call was to the woman I was with when I entered recovery. We'd been together a few years during my "hitting bottom" period and the first year of my sobriety. She just laughed at me over the phone and said, "I don't even think you're an alcoholic; you're just an asshole!" I replied, "I'm sure you're right about the asshole part, but I assure you I'm a *real* alcoholic." When I hung up the phone I felt a sense of peace and happiness. I realized I felt the same after each call. Other peoples' reaction to my amends was none of my business. I was to make the effort; the results were in the hands of a Power greater than myself.

Strangely, many of the people I needed to apologize to seemed to just show up at the appropriate time and place.

FADE IN:

INT. - STATER BROS SUPERMARKET - DAY

MARC stands in check-out line. Recognizes man in line directly in front of him. It's J.R., a Buckaroo of *mid-degree*. Marc owes him amends.

MARC

J.R! How ya doing?

J.R.

Uh…o.k. , I guess. Haven't seen you for a while. What'cha up to?

MARC

I don't go to bars anymore. Had to get in the Program. I owe you an amends for the hole in your wall.

J.R.

What hole?

MARC

Remember the night I blew a big hole in your living- room wall with my shotgun? The blast penetrated into the condo next door.

J.R.

Oh, shit; we all did stuff like that. I barely remember.

MARC

You must've paid someone to patch the hole. How much did it cost?

179

J.R.

(irritated) Nah, forget it. I don't even remember, to tell you the truth. Hey, did you hear about Shorty?

MARC

The old guy in the cowboy hat from Dick's Horseshoe? He sweeps the parking lot for complementary drinks at six every morning.

J.R.

Yeah. He died. No more free drinks for Shorty. They had a little service for him at Dick's and then scattered his ashes in the parking lot.

MARC

Wow! Does it get any cooler than that?

FADE OUT

Chapter 50

RIDING THE BUS

I didn't drive a car during my early sobriety. I refused to get a new driver's license for almost two years, long after the suspension of my license had been lifted. I walked or rode the bus. At first I was ashamed to ride the bus. After a while I adjusted and became One with the other bus riders. We were the salt of the earth, the oppressed bottom of the working class. We were the physically disabled and the mentally challenged.

Southern California has terrible public transportation. It can take up to four hours to travel from a location in South Orange County to a destination in North Orange County – one way. The same trip takes less than an hour by car. One rides the bus in Orange County only as a last resort. I became arrogant, proud to ride the bus. I didn't need to buy a car, or obtain the expensive high-risk insurance necessary for those of us victimized by our drunk driving arrests. I didn't need to go kiss the *man*'s ass at the DMV. I didn't need to feed a car environmentally incorrect petroleum products. I was a bus person.

Chapter 51

VOLUNTEER SERVICES

In 1983, I was coming up on two years clean and sober. My co-workers at the machine shop were amazed at the changes in my personality and behavior. A few guys started hanging around my work station at break-time and before work. They wanted to talk about my sobriety and my new mellow attitude. No more vodka and orange juice slushies. No more throwing spherical steel bearings at the clock when time wasn't moving fast enough for me. I began to experience a burning desire to be of service – to give back.

I called Orange County Volunteer Services. After an orientation process, I was assigned to volunteer a minimum of five hours a week at a County mental health clinic. I had no training, no experience, and no education. At first, they just let me talk informally with a few late stage winos – clients at the County's Alcoholism Services section. I enjoyed it. The Service Chief of our Alcoholism Services team encouraged me to sign up for a two year training program at University of California, Irvine. I would also be required to complete a two thousand hour supervised internship. I quit my quality control inspector job at the machine shop, went back to school, and became an alcohol and drug counselor.

Chapter 52

CAR OMEN

I *needed* a car to get to my classes at U.C.I. Many of the classes were held in the evening. I could get to U.C.I. on the bus, but there was no bus service available to get home at night. I was given a used car. It had major mechanical problems, but I was allowed to drive it as long as I could keep it running. I obtained the expensive high-risk insurance required by the *man*, and received my new driver's license.

My first class at U.C.I. was held in the evening. I think it was called "Alcoholism, the Individual, and Society". The car broke down about two miles from the campus. I took it as an omen I should drop out of school immediately and return to the machine shop. In reality, I was afraid to go back to school at age 41. I was afraid the decades of alcohol and drug abuse had damaged my brain to such an extent I wouldn't be able to retain information. I was also aware most of the other students in the counselor training program had advanced degrees. Many were already social workers, marriage and family therapists, and psychologists. Several M.D.s were enrolled in the program. They all wanted certification in addiction counseling. I felt very intimidated by my classmates' scholastic histories. My little support system of loved ones, the volunteer supervisor and Service Chief at the County clinic, and my own therapist convinced me to fix the car and stay with the U.C.I. program. They were right. Within a few weeks, I was much more comfortable with my classmates. I stayed with the program, received good grades, completed my internship, and received my certificates from U.C.I.

Chapter 53

BREAKIN' INTO OTHER PEOPLE'S STUFF

My first real, paid counseling job was in a hospital in Long Beach. It was a fifty bed medical model detox and recovery treatment center. The patients typically undergo three to five days in detox, plus twenty-eight days of recovery. The recovery program offered daily AA meetings, alcohol and drug education, group therapy and individual counseling. My job description was "line counselor". I was given a caseload of 5-7 patients to manage on an individual basis. I also had to do group counseling. The hospital employed about ten line counselors, day shift and night shift supervisors, an intake counselor, a program director, an M.D. and two R.N.s. We worked twelve-hour shifts; day shifts and night shifts. When I was hired, I was told I'd have every other weekend off, and co-facilitators for all my groups. I don't remember a weekend off, and I had to run all my groups alone. This was a completely new environment for me. Most of the patients were heroin and cocaine addicts, in addition to being alcoholics. Many came from the lumpen-proletariat criminal element of Long Beach and South Los Angeles. I was nervous and insecure all the time. My old County mental health team had been a little family. This place was hardcore. My training at the County and U.C.I. hadn't prepared me for Redgate Hospital.

My first group session was an "exit group", consisting of eleven patients scheduled to graduate within the next two weeks. My objective was to get the group to explore new ways of living on the "outside" without alcohol or other drugs. I thought, "I like to have fun in sobriety, so I'll get them to talk about things they used to do for fun before they became involved with drugs and alcohol". I nervously asked the group to think back to when they were little kids. What did they like to do? How did they get high naturally? Silence. Long, uncomfortable silence. My face felt flushed. My scalp itched. My mouth was dry. I wanted to run away. Finally, one guy shared. "I liked to break into people's stuff!" He was completely serious. Another patient chimed in, "Hey, me too. I liked to break into people's stuff, too. It was a real high!" The group was out of control.

I lasted about four months at Redgate Hospital, then moved on to my next counseling job.

Chapter 54

BLACK MASON

Redgate Hospital was located near my old drinking territory, in a rough area of Long Beach. We called it "the corner of Hooker and Crack Streets". Saturday mornings, on my way to work, I'd drive around the old neighborhood, listening to "Nothin' But the Blues", a local FM blues program. Traditional Delta blues, blasting from my car radio, provided an appropriate soundtrack to the sights of the Ghetto. Every Saturday morning I noticed a group of well-dressed African-American men congregating in front of an old building on Atlantic Avenue – right across the street from where Eddie's Sandbox stood ten years previously. This was 1985, and Eddie's was no more. I decided to investigate. I parked the car on Atlantic, and walked over to the guys standing in front of the building. They were obviously Black Freemasons, and the old building was a Masonic Lodge. I introduced myself as a former member of a Masonic Lodge in Columbus, Nebraska. I told them I had opposed segregated lodges and had "stopped paying dues twenty years ago". The Master of the Lodge told me to come back the following Saturday at seven in the morning, and "wear a suit and tie".

The following Saturday I showed up at the appropriate time, wearing a borrowed suit and tie. I was nervous and uncomfortable. One of the lodge brothers escorted me into a small room, where I proved to his satisfaction I was indeed a Master Mason. He told me to remain where I was and someone would come for me in due time. Soon, another brother came for me. He directed me to follow him into the Lodge. I was placed alone in the center of the room. The Master of the Lodge ordered me to introduce myself to the Brothers, and explain my purpose in being there. I related my Masonic history, my opposition to segregated lodges, and my desire to be a part of *their* lodge.

They took a vote – right there in front of me! My old Nebraska lodge voted on new candidates in secret. One "black ball", or "no" vote, would bar the candidate from membership in the Lodge. The candidate would not be present during the vote. The vote was unanimous. I was now a member of St. John's Lodge #23 in Long Beach, California, the only white guy in an all black Masonic Lodge.

Chapter 55

DRUG DIVERSION

Immediately after leaving Redgate Hospital, I was hired to supervise and facilitate three adult felony drug diversion groups in Orange County – Costa Mesa, Huntington Beach, and Mission Viejo. Drug diversion clients were all court/probation referrals. Most had been arrested for felony drug possession. Drug diversion was a way these folks could escape a felony conviction. They simply had to attend ten consecutive weekly groups and one eight-hour Saturday workshop to keep a felony-free record. Airline pilots, stock brokers, attorneys – anyone whose livelihood depended upon a clean police record – all could keep their licenses and continue their careers.

My work with drug offenders naturally brought me into professional contact with probation and law enforcement officers. It was strange, yet somehow natural, to be working full-time on the "law and order" side of the fence. I participated in night shift ride-alongs with the Costa Mesa and Laguna Beach Police Departments, and the Hays County, Texas Sheriff's Department. I completed a short training course on Domestic Violence Counseling with the Orange County Probation Department, and graduated from the Laguna Beach Police Department's Citizens Academy.

ORANGE SUNSHINE

My denial has lifted. The Great Truth I've always secretly known, yet feared, has burst into consciousness. I am *The Man!*

Chapter 56

INDIA

I made my first visit to India in October 1994. My destination was the India-Pakistan border, and an ashram associated with my spiritual path. The ashram is home to a Perfect Living Master, the Successor to the Saint who initiated me in 1975. Sobriety made it possible for me to get back to my spiritual practice – meditation and a lacto-vegetarian diet.

While in India, I met people from all over the world. I was especially interested in talking with people from countries formerly occupied by the old Soviet Union. A small group of us would meet in the ashram kitchen every morning at five-thirty. We'd drink Indian tea, chop vegetables, and discuss matters spiritual and mundane. One morning, after my third big cup of *chai,* I entertained the group by relating some of my war stories from the Communist Party Marxist-Leninist days. A young woman from Romania looked at me with a very serious face and said, with flat affect, "It must have been very easy to be radical socialist in Hollywood, U.S.A. in nineteen seventies."

I'm still laughing.

ABOUT THE AUTHOR

Marc DuQuette was born in 1942 in Long Beach, California where he and his younger brother, author Lon Milo DuQuette were raised until they moved to Nebraska. Marc graduated from Columbus High School in Columbus, Nebraska in 1960. He served in U.S. Army Infantry, Army Reserve, and Nebraska National Guard and received an Honorable Discharge in December 1967

During the 1960's and 1970's, he pushed life to the limits as an alcoholic outlaw biker in Costa Mesa, California, an acid-dropping, commune living hippie, and a communist political radical. For most of 1968 he lived in the woods of Southern Oregon and subsequently became involved in various radical groups such as Vietnam Veterans Against the War, the Cuban based Venceremos Brigade, and the Maoist October League/Communist Party Marxist-Leninist, from which he was ultimately expelled for being drunk at an International Womens Day rally in San Francisco. In order to make a living to support his "lifestyle" he worked at various factory jobs and pretended to organize the workers.

In 1979 and 1980, Marc picked up two DUIs and refused to attend Alcoholics Anonymous (AA) meetings at the court's request. As a result, he was sentenced to Orange County Main Jail.

On December 19, 1981 Marc hit rock bottom. He had a spiritual experience and called the Central Office of a Twelve Step Program. He attended his first meeting over 27 years ago and started working the Twelve Steps. He has maintained continuous sobriety and still attends meetings and works the steps to this day.

After becoming sober, Marc dedicated his life to helping others overcome their addictions. In 1983, he started volunteering five hours a week at the Orange County Health Care Agency – Alcoholism Services, and ultimately quit his factory job (and pretense of organizing workers) to take a two year Certification

Program at the University of California, Irvine. He completed a supervised internship at the Orange Country Health Care Agency: Alcoholism, Mental Health and Drug Abuse. He has worked detox and recovery - medical model and social model - and facilitated groups as well as supervised felony drug diversion programs.

Marc continues to work with alcoholics/addicts and codependents, who also must actively attend and participate in the twelve step programs "appropriate to their needs." He does private consultations only with clients who are personally referred.

ORANGE SUNSHINE: How I Almost Survived America's Cultural Revolution, is Marc's first book and chronicles his experiences through the turbulent sixties, through his addictions and brushes with the law, and ultimately to his spiritual awakening and sense of purpose. He currently lives in the beautiful Hill Country near Austin, Texas, and frequently travels to India to recharge his spiritual batteries.

For more information, photos, and insights about Marc and ***ORANGE SUNSHINE***, visit his website at:

www.marcduquette.com

Marc can also be contacted at:

Marc DuQuette
P.O. BOX 1313
Dripping Springs, TX 78620-1313

marc@marcduquette.net

Made in the USA
Las Vegas, NV
08 February 2021